POWERFUL RESILIENCE

A Memoir

DR. KIMBERLY LEVERETTE

With Dr. Joyce Putnam & Dr. Sharon Schwille

Published by So It Is Written, LLC
Detroit, MI
SoItIsWritten.net

Powerful Resilience: A Memoir
Copyright © 2022 by by Kimberly Leverette with Sharon A. Schwille and Joyce G. Putnam

Edited by: So It Is Written – www.SoItIsWritten.net

Formatting: Ya Ya Ya Creative – www.YaYaYaCreative.com

ISBN: 979-8-9861260-1-2

LCCN: 2022909042

PRINTED AND BOUND IN THE UNITED STATES OF AMERICA

TO MAYA,
MY SUPERSTAR

ACKNOWLEDGMENTS

Thank you, Dr. Sharon Schwille, for asking me to share my life story.

To everyone who has worked with me over the last ten years, I express my enormous message of appreciation to you. You are an invaluable group of people who made it possible for me to complete a memoir. Because of all your distinct roles, you all helped me to finish my book. All of our roles changed over the ten years it took me to bring closure to the process. During the entire time, all of you continued to support my struggles and successes.

When we began, Dr. Sharon Schwille and I talked Dr. Joyce Putnam into joining us, resulting in a team of three. In the beginning, their roles were interviewing, listening, writing, editing and asking me questions about things they did not understand. My role was thinking, remembering, talking, and challenging and correcting misunderstandings and perspectives.

Thank you, Dr. Carol Sharp, Dr. Sonya Gunnings-Moton, Dr. John Schwille and Mr. Jimmy Putnam, for providing feedback about the draft we shared with you. The feedback provided the basis for our team to consider major changes in the structure of my story and we moved from a story about me to a memoir.

This change provided the foundation for me to tell the team about the loss of my voice.

I was heard and our team of three once again focused on a successful finished copy. Thank you, Dr. John Schwille for your contributions to editing. Thank you to my family and friends. Dad would be so proud! Without your continued support and nagging me to get busy and do the work necessary for my story to be told through my voice, it would have taken me years to achieve what is now completed. Special thanks to my sister, Katrina for her blessing.

Thank you, Kathy B., Kathy R., Nat, Henri, Joyce, Jimmy, and Sonya for being my mentors.

Thank you to all educators who stand on the front line for children every day!

TABLE OF CONTENTS

There was never any real expectation of who or what I would become.
So, I decided to run until I finally soared!

Kimberly as a child

INTRODUCTION

My story was written for high school and college students who might be experiencing tough times in school and life. Please understand that you are not alone. Mentors, education and self-awareness are a few key takeaways the reader will find as each encounter in life will shape and define your true purpose. Tough times don't last; tough people do!

My story was written to provide an inside point of view for adults working with and mentoring students who live in poverty. It takes an intimate look into how mentoring relationships with young people can help to shape, transform and influence lives in powerful ways.

My story was written for broken families like mine, where generations of alcoholism and mental illness can create a vicious cycle. We must break the curse, forgive and heal.

PROLOGUE

I grew up in dire poverty with three siblings and an unstable mother who was severely mentally ill and an alcoholic. As a result, for the most part, I raised myself. All four of us children spent time in five foster homes (not always together) and at least half a dozen times with relatives. This meant that we changed schools at least ten times. My sister, youngest brother and I lived in the final foster home, where we were finally adopted by our foster parents.

Hurt, heartbreak and healing led me to opportunity, optimism, hope for the future, and finally, a successful adult life. Despite all of the hardships I faced growing up, I triumphed over each obstacle and attained both academic and professional achievements. Out of the trenches of life, I became an exemplary teacher, principal and central administrator of schools. My siblings, mother and relatives all came to depend on me as the stabilizing person in the family.

I am a runner. I have always run physically, emotionally, and psychologically. Sometimes, my motivation was to run from something and sometimes to something. Running physically makes me feel energized, invigorated and in control of myself. Emotionally, I run in response to a sense of being unloved and yearning for my mother to simply say, "I love you." I ran toward possibilities of lasting love, but when I found a spouse, I ran from him as well. Psychologically, my running is a way to escape images of myself being less than adequate. At the same time, I ran toward opportunities—usually, professional ones, to continue my growth and sense of self-control.

I've learned that memoirs that expose the hardships of poverty, alcoholism, addiction, deprivation and other adversities are numerous. Books such as *Teacher Man* (Frank McCourt, 2006), *The Glass Castle* (Jeannette Walls, 2009), *Hill Billy Elegy* (J. D. Vance, 2016), *High Achiever* (Tiffany Jenkins, 2017), *Educated* (Tara Westover, 2018), *Notes from a Young Black Chef: A Memoir* (Kwame Onwuachi with Joshua David Stein, 2019) and *The Yellow House: A Memoir* (Sarah M. Broom) invite the reader to vicariously live through often unimaginable circumstances and events while achieving success in many aspects of life, nevertheless. My story adds to this rich collection. It is unique because each person who lives in extreme conditions of poverty and abuse is shaped by their circumstances in unique ways.

In sharing my story, I aspire to give inspiration, hope, vision and courage to those who come from deprived circumstances to push her or himself out and away from deprivation—emotionally, psychologically, and even physically when possible. My story aims to provide tactics such as recognizing and taking advantage of opportunities presented by potential mentors, obtaining as much education as possible and exercising self-control over temptations such as drugs, alcohol or relationship abuse. Ideally, readers accustomed to conditions similar to mine will find the strength, courage, and determination to govern their situations, forge a purposeful, energizing life for themselves, and make a difference by helping another person achieve personal and professional success.

For more fortunate readers who did not endure such hardships, *Powerful Resilience* will paint a vivid picture of my life in the hopes that they will not only have empathy for people who've endured harsh conditions, but also be inspired to find ways to support people who need guidance during their personal and professional growth. My story highlights the importance of mentors "having my back" and pushing me up the ladders of psychological, educational, and financial success. Our hope is that readers will look for opportunities to become a mentor to someone on a journey like mine.

Chapter 1

GROWING PAINS

I see my mother; I see myself. I thought my mom was beautiful, and I still do. I possess many of her characteristics. For instance, I look just like her. I have her somewhat Asian-shaped eyes and her easy smile—my sister does, too. We share the same cocoa brown skin color. I also have a lot of her personality. She has a hell of a sense of humor. She's so funny. I am, too. She can tell a delightful story about growing up. She's a likable person. People love her because she takes an interest in everyone.

On the other side, my mother had other qualities, such as drinking too much and being gone for days at a time when I was young. She had severe psychological problems and battled alcoholism, which meant periods of hospitalization throughout my childhood and up to the present time. It wasn't until many, many years later that I knew and understood what happened to her when she had an attack. She had no control of her thoughts and actions and withdrew into a psychotic state. And that's where we differ.

It wasn't a given that I would come this far in my life—earning several degrees, including a doctorate and securing highly-responsible positions in school districts. Yet, as I look back, I know that my work in these various places positively affected the learning of both students and teachers alike. Under the circumstances in which I grew up, most people who know me may have predicted that I might not finish high school, much less work in a well-respected job that paid more than minimum wage. But I did. It wasn't easy, but my ambition and help from mentors along the way allowed me to achieve a success that was difficult to imagine when I was young.

Born in Pensacola, Florida, on January 19, 1971, my mom named me Kimberly Leverette. I never knew my father or anything about him; I only have a vague memory of my mother telling me that his mother was a teacher. Teaching is in my blood due to my father's side. Although I asked many times, my mother never responded to my questions about my father. In fact, she never identified him by name. I have a hunch he was in the Navy since there is a base there, but my mom didn't even tell me that.

I am the second child born of four children to Janice Faye. I remember being called "Faye's kids." My mother was always called by her middle name. None of us have the same father. My younger sister and younger brother met their fathers, but they don't have a relationship with them—they just know who they are. My older brother doesn't know and doesn't care to find out about his father, but I've always been curious about mine. I have chosen not to do a DNA test to check out my ancestry related to my father. Simply, I do not have the emotional energy to do this at this point in my life. My two younger siblings and I finally got a father figure when we were adopted by a couple who wanted to keep us from aging out of foster care. Unfortunately, my older brother Ray was already too old to qualify for foster care by that time, so he was not adopted. Instead, he continued to raise himself while always remaining in contact with the three of us younger kids.

When I was about two or three, my mom moved our young family of three to the Midwest to a small city named Flint, Michigan. Unfortunately, she started having psychotic episodes on top of her excessive drinking. My mom wanted to be near her extended family, who lived in Flint. Although I remember little of my early childhood in Flint, I do recall people talking about my mother. They said things like, "That woman is crazy. Stay away if she just sits there and looks like she's in her own world." If she said to stay away from her, people did just that. I can't imagine the darkness and despair she experienced as she suffered in the isolation of her mind.

As an adult, I gained access to my mother's medical records. In addition to being an alcoholic, I learned that my mother was diagnosed as bipolar, paranoid, and schizophrenic with depression. Because of her frequent hospitalizations, I grew up in many different foster homes and homes of relatives. I visited my mother when she was in an institution because our social worker would take us to see her occasionally. I was always excited at the prospect of seeing my mom, and she was excited about seeing us. When we visited, we would try to cheer her up. She was quiet from her sedation, but she would smile and seemed very tired. We just sat for about half an hour. I could tell she wanted to go home with us, but I also knew there was no way she could take care of us like a normal mother.

We kids were baptized at Canaan Baptist Church. Sometimes, we went to Sunday school. I have a picture of my sister and me dressed up in our Easter Sunday outfits. One of my aunts came over and fixed up my mom so she could look nice for church. The church became a place of comfort for me. Now, I am a member of that same church because it feels like home to me, and God's words comfort me.

When I was young, my mother never showed me typical signs of love. Without these overt signs, I grew up wondering whether my mother really loved me. I certainly don't remember my mother hugging me or telling me she loved me. Not having my mother consistently at home and being in so many different foster homes made me feel like I never belonged anywhere. Even though I was a popular kid who belonged to the "in" crowd at school and was active in many school activities, I still had this emotional hole—a feeling of emptiness and not really fitting in. Those feelings followed me throughout my teenage years and into my adult life.

As a first grader, I was already a reader. When times were good at home, my mother and older brother worked with me on reading, spelling and math in my early school years. We didn't have many books, but we could bring some home from school. My mother was always reading the Bible, which gave me the sense that reading was important. Even today, my mother reads the Bible she keeps on an end table. She also answers the door and spends time with the Jehovah's Witnesses whenever they come by. She told me, "It doesn't matter who I talk to about the Bible—the story never changes." I cherish the memories of those few times when Mom would read with me.

During those elementary school years, times were difficult when my mother started getting sick. I didn't know how to deal with these situations. My mom would just sit in a stupor, moaning and rocking back and forth. Her alcoholism also played into the situation. I now realize that in my family, people don't just die of diabetes or heart disease; they kill themselves from drinking. But with my mom, it was even worse because of her mental illness.

Due to the effects of her alcoholism and mental illness, we had to grow up quickly. My mother left me and my siblings at home alone quite often, so my oldest brother had a lot of responsibility for taking care of us. He did a fairly decent job of it. He taught me how to tie my shoes and zip my coat. There were times when we woke up in the morning and Mom wasn't there. I didn't know where she was. It was my brother who had to get up and get everyone ready for school.

"Up and at 'em," he'd say. "School starts in one hour, and you have to dress and brush your teeth!"

My sister and I would crawl out of bed as my older brother ironed our clothes for school and yelled, "We have to get out of here. If we miss the bus, we won't have a ride to school." He taught us how to iron, wash dishes, wash our clothes and hang them up to dry, so they were ready to wear the next day. We did not have a washer and dryer. We used our great-grandma's old washboard, which we put in the bathtub, and washed our clothes there.

My mom was a good cook when she was well. Her specialties were meat loaf, chicken and noodles, pork chops and gravy, ham hocks and greens. We'd get a plate, dish up our food and sit at the table to eat together. But whenever she fell apart, so did our lives.

My Aunt Marilyn was our saving grace. Our foster families allowed her to take us out to the beach close to town. It was a wonderful place for picnics and playing in the water. We would stick our feet in the water since we didn't know how to swim, but we had fun. Unfortunately, we didn't have many good times like that.

We lived for periods of time in several different foster homes and with relatives several times. Each time my mother's health improved, she went to court to regain legal custody of us. Often, we were back with our mother for about nine months to a year before she had another breakdown. However, her breakdowns resulted in our being taken away by the state and placed in another foster home or living with relatives. She wanted us back as a family, although now I realize that when we were together, her dependency on alcohol seemed to be the most important relationship in her life, not her children. She was an alcoholic, so she was either drunk or hung over.

I was not embarrassed about being in a foster home because the bottom line was, no matter what Mama did, she kept going back and forth to court to get us back. I always hoped that she would stop drinking, not get sick anymore and just be okay. But it would happen repeatedly, and my brothers, sister, and I would go back into foster care. Finally, it reached a point where our own family, her own relatives—my aunts, uncles, cousins—didn't want to take "those kids." It felt like an insult to Mama and me. I didn't care what anybody said about our family; I always wanted to be with my mom.

I cared a lot about what others said about my mother. As a child, I heard the adults whispering and knew they were talking about my mom. Then, they would turn around and smile in my face as though I didn't know what they were saying or like I was invisible. I wished I could use my kid voice to tell them exactly how I felt, but I swallowed that voice and remained silent. Kids are so much smarter and more resilient than they are given credit for, especially children who dealt with trauma. It's exceedingly difficult to be disingenuous with them. I used to think, *One day, I will show them! I'll tell them they shouldn't talk about my mother being sick and not being able to take care of herself, much less her kids.* I wanted to be proud of my mother and defend her. Still, it wasn't easy when I knew other people were talking about her problematic behaviors. Eventually, the court took her parental rights away.

Despite the absences and hardships, I never backed away from having a relationship with my mother. I learned how to drive while in college. So, I always tried to visit her in the hospital and her home. From the day I was born and even now as a middle-aged adult, the child inside me always wants to be with my mother and yearns for her love. I have spent so much time working hard for my mother's approval, wanting and just wanting my family to be together. I never stopped hoping that I could keep our family functioning normally. However, I got tired because no one else helped or seemed to care—not my siblings or relatives. They all had their own problems—mostly with alcohol. In fact, just recently, my uncle—drunk as usual— was out dancing in the street and got hit by two cars.

School was my safe haven. I attended several elementary schools because I lived in different foster homes. So even though I had a lot of emotional baggage, I could set it aside while I immersed myself in everything the school had to offer. In spite of my academic difficulties, I became engrossed in learning and interacting with my classmates. That was my identity. For instance, when we lived with The Smiths—our fourth foster parents, I didn't feel like I was part of their family. They didn't take an interest in what I liked to do and didn't talk much while we had dinner. They just wanted the money for taking in foster kids. But I went to school, and it was okay. I felt safe there and could lose myself during the school day.

Sometimes, my mother wasn't in any state to send us to school, especially when she was hung over in the morning. So, we just got up and went to school. One time, my mother burned down the house we were living in at the time, so we went to my great grandma's. In fact, my mom set fires in several of the places we lived, but we were never hurt. When this happened, we were sent to foster homes during my mother's hospitalization. My siblings and I were usually split up because the foster homes couldn't take us all. I never had to stay by myself, but my older brother and sister did. The trauma of sibling separation made me angry and sad.

When we attended Williams Elementary, Mom would come up to the school for parent/teacher conferences. Of course, I got kicked out of school a couple of times. During my third-grade year, I fought another student on the bus, which continued even after we got to our bus stop. I was never the aggressor, but I'd fight back in a minute. I would come to school and be argumentative. My mother told me, "If somebody hits you, hit him back!" So, I did. Then, she would have to come to school and be a mothering advocate for me. She did that for all three of us whenever she was stable enough to get to school.

I was a great reader and writer in school; however, math was difficult. Several years ago, I had an opportunity to look at my school transcripts. I noticed how I consistently got bad grades in math from elementary school all the way through high school. In the sixth grade, I was held back, and it was, of course, for math. I felt like I was dumb and especially not good at math. I was thinking, given everything I'd already been through, if math was the thing that I was beating myself up for, I needed to just let it go. I thought, *Wow! I could have really been a dynamic student if I had had those foundational math skills that I missed in elementary school.* There were so many gaps in my learning from moving back and forth between Mama's, the foster homes, and relatives because each move required a school change. I understand how these gaps in my learning occurred. As an educator, I take action in the schools where I work to decrease the learning gaps for my students and set students up for success.

I was also a Title I student when I got into the upper grades. The school district received federal funds based on the percentage of children living at or below the poverty level. I was one of those students. This meant I received intervention help with schoolwork if I needed it. For example, I needed help with math. I went to summer school to learn the math concepts and skills I needed to pass the sixth grade. I rode my bike back and forth to Longfellow Middle School, where I took the math classes and finally met the math objectives. When I went to middle school that Fall, I was placed in the grade that I was supposed to be in—

the seventh grade. However, during the seventh and eighth grades, I moved back and forth between Bryant and Longfellow Middle Schools. I felt as though I just slogged my way through these middle school years, keeping a low profile and making average grades. Mama continued to have psychotic episodes exacerbated by her drinking, and we were in foster homes much of the time. I was always worried about her while getting used to being in yet another home that wasn't really mine.

Chapter 2
FINDING A DAD

Running was a great outlet for me; I loved running. Running kept me focused and healthy. It gave me a powerful sense of self as I became a teenager. In middle school, I ran track and cross country. I was on the track team in high school. I ran long-distance races—the two-mile run, the mile, and the half-mile run. I was definitely not a sprinter! I was named the most improved several times and became co-captain of the team. This position allowed me to develop my leadership skills. I also became good friends with the girls on the team who had home issues similar to mine—single-parent households where alcohol and drugs were a way of life. We developed a sense of community, a sense of belonging.

Being on the track team taught me discipline. I learned the value of practice and preparation in anticipation of a track meet. As I found out how mentally tough and intimidating the other team could be, I learned to keep going in spite of it. I learned teamwork, cooperation, and respect for my coach and teammates. I did not win all of my races, but I did win my share of medals. I never ran a race I did not finish. To me, finishing was winning.

Even today, I still have a deep love for running because it gives me a way to work out my physical, mental and emotional issues. It gives me time to think through problems, sort out my options and decide what to do. It reduces all the stress that builds up during the day. Years ago, someone asked me, "What are you running from?" I was taken aback and had to think about the question.

"I'm running from the pressure I feel to take care of my mom plus my brothers and sister when they get in trouble. I'm running from the tension I have because I'm not happy with my own personal life," I responded. I now realize that if something wasn't working in my personal life, it wasn't worth my worrying about because I didn't have the knowledge or skills to fix the problem. Rather than get upset and frustrated because I couldn't figure out how to change a situation, I learned to let it go. For instance, when my sisters got pregnant and moved out on their own, I was scared for them. But I knew I couldn't change the choices they made about their own lives.

Now that I'm older, my perspective has changed. If someone asked me why I'm running today, I would respond, "I am not running from anything! I am taking responsibility for every right and wrong action in my life. I am in charge.

I'm done running from emotional baggage. I am standing in my true sense of self!" This helps me not only to avoid creating problems but to also solve them. Now, I am thinking about where I am running to.

During my eighth-grade year, I had to move from the foster home I was in because my foster dad made advances toward me. When a foster sister told me he was harassing her, I called our social worker.

"Our foster dad is asking me to play a touching game, and he would give us money," I reported to the social worker. "You need to pick us up and get us out of here!"

The social worker took us to the A&W on the corner of Pierson and Clio Roads, and I told her what had happened. After that, things moved fast. We went right back and packed our bags that same night. I don't remember exactly where we went that night. It was a "safe house" for abused kids, but we didn't return to that foster home. Although I was just a middle school kid, I had a lot of street smarts and common sense. I knew right from wrong. I had to protect myself and my sister. After a day or two, we ended up in another foster home, but this one was different. Our foster parents cared for us like we were their own.

I had a lot of great teachers while living in Flint. After going to several different elementary and middle schools, once I got to Flint Northwestern High School, things became more stable for me. I completed all four years in one school—making for an unusually favorable situation for me. I got comfortable and developed a sense of security, knowing what to expect every day at school. The same kids tended to be in each of my classes, and most of the teachers knew my family situation and took an interest in helping me do well at school.

When I was in ninth grade, the case worker came for her regular visit with our foster family, The Jacksons. It was just us three younger kids, and we were doing well. Ray had aged out of the foster care system.

"How are you all getting along?" The case worker asked. The Jacksons' response surprised us.

"We'd like to adopt these three kids. We think they are great kids and pretty soon, they will age out of the system. We think they should stay with us instead of having to make another move somewhere."

At that point, the people at the foster care agency were going back and forth on whether or not they were going to send me to a girls' home in Detroit because I was getting older and would soon be too old for the foster care system. Even as a ninth grader, I was full of anger, resentment, bitterness, and rage. All of those emotions boiled inside me. I felt abandoned by my mother, and due to the lack of money, we didn't have many toys or books like the other kids in school had. It felt like I was not as worthy as my classmates. The Jacksons intervened by adopting my sister, my younger brother, and me so we could stay together with them. When we moved to foster homes over the years, usually, we did not get to stay together. This was the best place the three of us could be; we were together. The Jacksons adopted other kids I have not kept up a relationship with. Instead, I stay in close touch with my birth mother, birth sister, and brothers, who live in Flint.

Since my older brother had already aged out of the system, he couldn't be adopted. At the time, he lived with either an aunt, a friend, or whoever could house him at the time. He and his longtime girlfriend moved in together and started their own family. Eventually, he returned to live with our birth mother.

My adoptive father was quite a man—larger than life. He came into my life as a foster dad when I was thirteen and adopted me about a year after. From the first day we met him, I called him "Dad." I never called any other men "Dad." Mr. Jackson was the real thing—the dad I had always wanted. I felt like his daughter, and none of us ever thought differently. Sadly, Dad died several years ago, and I miss him greatly.

When The Jacksons adopted us, they changed our last name to theirs—Jackson. But this did not sit well with me. I didn't want people to know I was adopted. I wanted my friends and my teachers to think that I came from a "normal" family with a loving mother who took good care of us. I was fourteen when I was adopted, so it wasn't like I was a little girl who didn't have an identity. I felt like I was going to lose that identity—*my name.* My name was the one thing I could claim as something I was born with that belonged solely to me. Everything else about my identity— my biological mom, a stable place to live, a stable school, friendships built over the years—were all taken away from me. I had no choice in those decisions.

So, when I told my teachers that I was adopted, I asked them to call me Kimberly Leverette Jackson to keep my birth name as part of my full name. And they did—they respected me. So then, I told my friends that my mom had gotten married, and that's why my last name was Jackson on the school records. However, I wanted them to call me Kimberly Leverette because that's how they knew me, and I liked it that way. That was just me trying to survive and do what kids do—creating my own identity, my own space, and place in the world.

Being adopted helped me have four good years in high school, even though I still had a lot of anger inside. I continued to be strong-willed in high school, not wanting others to tell me what to do. I wanted to do things *my way*—like keeping Leverette as my last name. As a teenager going through growth and puberty, I was trying to figure out who I was emotionally and psychologically. Besides running track, I started running in a separate way. I ran away from home many times in high school. I wanted to do things my own way, and my adoptive mother usually didn't agree. She would tell me I needed to change my skirt because it was too short. She would tell me to change my attitude as I was yelling too much. Because I felt she was picking on me, I resented it.

My biological mother never was really out of the picture. She visited us at The Jacksons, but she still lived a traumatic and dramatic life. One night while she and her boyfriend, Rus, were partying and drinking too much, Rus stabbed her all the way down her chest from her breastbone to below her naval. My mother had to be hospitalized and cared for even after being released until she healed. My oldest brother stayed with her during this time, but I checked on her, too. These experiences are part of the reason I ran away. I needed time away from all the changes that resulted from being sent to foster homes, leaving me feeling angry because we couldn't live with my mom like a typical family. My life was so different from most of my friends who at least had a stable family. My life wasn't normal, and many of its people were not normal either.

Whenever I ran away, I went to a friend's place, my aunt's house, or called Kathy, the track coach with who I had a great relationship. Each time I did this, Dad came and found me. He listened to me, talked with me and then I went back home. I knew I was breaking his heart.

"Co-Co (he called me Co-Co for short), I love you, and I don't want you in the streets," he said. Although I saw the pain in his eyes, I was just too angry with my adoptive mom and angry about not being able to be with my birth mother. My adoptive mom and I were always at odds because I was so stubborn, and she wasn't my real mom.

"Co-Co, you need to clean your room!" she'd say sharply. I would respond by turning my back, stomping off, and slamming my door. No one could replace my real mom. But Dad was always there, understanding me and supporting me. For instance, when I ran around the neighborhood for practice and emotional relief, he followed me around in the car to make sure I was safe. He never gave up on me. He didn't replace my biological dad because I never knew my real dad or anything about him. But Dad was the only foster father who I felt really cared about me.

Dad impacted my life in many ways, even with his work ethic. He had worked at General Motors for over thirty years. He came from Arkansas in 1968 with only a fourth-grade education. He had to stay home, take care of the family, and work in the fields rather than go to school in those days. When he became a teenager, he went north to find a job. He moved to Flint, walked into General Motors, found a job, and stayed on the line for over thirty years. That's how he provided a stable home and support for his family, including two kids of his own and five adopted kids. His friends would come over and visit him because he opened up our house to everyone. He always told me to work hard and wanted me to go to college to become an engineer. My dad never complained about his job. He was never late, and he never missed a day at GM.

"Co-Co, engineers are always needed, and you will make a lot of money at General Motors," Dad said to me. Of course, being on the line, he knew the engineers in the plant were college-educated and well paid. But actually, Dad didn't really care what I majored in. He just hoped that I would go to college.

There weren't many white people who lived on the north side of Flint, where I lived. But one day here comes my dad with his friend from work—a white man—and they called each other "brother." He and my dad spent time together a lot. They shook hands, ate at the same dinner table, and hugged each other as great friends. My dad said, "There's a whole lot of racism in this world, and there are a whole lot of people who are not racists. Choose your side."

When I was in high school, I expected to enlist in the Army after I graduated to be trained and get a good-paying job after I left the military. But then my track coach talked to me and changed my whole life. After Christmas vacation, I was in the final semester of my senior year when my track coach, Coach Kathy, called me into her office.

"What do you plan to do after graduation?" She asked.

"I'm going to join the Army because it will give me something worthwhile to do. I can learn skills I need to get the kind of jobs where I would get paid well."

"No, you are not going into the Army," she said vehemently. "You are going to apply for college!" She told me that I had the academic ability and could manage college life and do well.

When I graduated from high school, I looked at my report card—I did manage to get my high school diploma. The diploma came with a record of all my school years. It had all these different schools listed on it where we had jumped around. I wished I had stayed in one school for at least a couple of years so I could have made some lasting friends. At least the four years in high school helped me build a few of those friendships.

I was surprised because no one had ever talked to me about college. Plus, college had never been an expectation or ambition while growing up. It simply was not part of the environment in which I lived. Growing up in poverty, moving through the foster system, then being adopted by foster parents who did not even have a high school education did not create a conducive atmosphere to dream about college. So, when Coach Kathy told me I would apply to college, I was taken aback. The only thing I thought to ask at the time was, "Where am I applying?"

"To Michigan State University!" Coach Kathy replied.

I didn't even know where that was. I had heard about Michigan State because Coach Kathy's husband attended there. She had talked about him and his getting a doctorate degree. But when Coach Kathy said that I should apply to college, I was so shocked that I didn't even remember what she had told me. Right away, Coach Kathy asked, "Well, what do you want to be?" I had no idea what I wanted to be if I didn't join the Army. Because I admired her and my teachers were an inspiration to me, I responded, "I want to be a teacher." After all, teachers and schools made me feel safe while growing up.

I thought about my African American friends who had gone off to college, who seemed smarter than me and had better opportunities than I've had—but weren't finishing their degrees. This was scary stuff that made me wonder if I should even try going to college. But Coach Kathy was very matter of fact and self-assured in communicating her belief in me.

"Kim, you can accomplish whatever you put your mind to, including getting a college education." I knew right then there was no way I would tell Coach Kathy, "No, I am not going to apply." So, I applied to Michigan State University plus a few other colleges within commuting distance. I also applied to a college in Ohio because my best friend was in college there. I got a letter of recommendation from Dr. Burtley, my track coach's husband. He was superintendent of Flint Schools at the time.

I had to draft an essay to apply to Michigan State and to the College Achievement Admission Program (CAAP), a program for first-generation, low-income college students. Since my high school grades were not great, I knew my essay had to be good. I also realized I had only one story to tell, which was my own life story. Once I made that decision, my heart was clear that I wanted to come back to the community and help children growing up as I did. I wrote about aspiring to be a teacher and my desire to return to an urban area to teach.

When you are writing about foster homes and being adopted because your mother can't take care of you, you're thinking, *"Are my life experiences a weakness?"* and *"I'm not going to get in."* I felt like college was for someone else. It was for kids who had the best grades and had been given opportunities that I did not have. I had to draft my essay with pen and paper—no computer, no spell check; but I was determined to be the best student I could be. Even though this seemed far out of reach for me, I took my chances and wrote about myself. I thought, "Anything's possible." So, I wrote that essay and never looked back. Coach Kathy read it and said, "This is perfect!"

This is perfect? Okay! I thought.

Normally, my adoptive parents would have thought anything I wrote was fantastic. But when I showed them my essay, they were not sure that I would be accepted. I worked really, really hard, and I wasn't under any pressure to get into the university like kids whose parents are college-educated. The essay was raw but from my heart. So, I sent it in, thinking to myself, *We'll see what happens.*

One day, I ran home, and I pushed the door open, shouting that my track team had won the meet that day. I ran the last lap of the 1600 (4 x 400) meter relay and the 1600-meter run. We had won both events.

"That's wonderful. But come here and open what came in the mail for you today!" My adoptive mother responded.

I noticed that the envelope was from Michigan State. I was accepted! I was both thrilled and scared. I was thrilled because I hadn't expected it and scared because I would now begin an unknown experience for which I wasn't prepared academically, socially, or psychologically. I was extremely excited, but I didn't connect with how huge the university was, what the College of Education program was and how it could change my life.

Now, I can look back at that time and realize there was a list of things that I wanted to happen in the back of my mind. For example, as far back as I can remember, I wanted my mother to say "I love you" to me. By the time I graduated from high school, she had never once said that to me. I also developed a fervent desire to know who my biological father was—what he was like and what he did for a living. It would have given me a more rooted sense of who I was. Then, there was my wish that my mother would get well, stop drinking and come home at night. I did not want to live in foster homes; I wanted to live with my mother. I didn't realize that moving ten to twelve times affected me. Before being adopted and having a permanent home, day-to-day things were also big on my wish list. I wanted food in the house, and I wanted some new clothes to wear. After being adopted, the one thing I wished for most of all was to change my last name back to my "real" name.

Chapter 3

COLLEGE LIFE

As I packed the few clothes and possessions I decided to take to college, I was terrified but excited. Besides clothes, I took some spiral notebooks for classes, a pillow, a hair dryer, and makeup. You'd think that because I've moved so many times while growing up, I'd be used to packing, but this was different. I had no idea what to expect. I'd seen the campus only once when I went to register and go on a campus tour led by an upperclassman. So here I was, leaving the only father figure I felt close to, my real mom and siblings. My stomach had more than its usual share of knots.

While Dad drove, I chatted nervously during the whole trip to the campus. "How big do you think my room will be? I forgot my hairspray. Will you call me when you get back home?"

"Co-Co, you'll find out when we get there. I know you'll be fine."

I was assigned to Brody Complex. I was stunned when I saw what Brody Complex looked like. It was solid red brick. I don't know what I was imagining, but it definitely wasn't anything so solid and imposing. I saw all the other cars—all newer than my dad's, white students with so much luggage that they needed help getting into the dorm. Some of them even had little refrigerators! I had two suitcases. I checked in, and a lady gave me a key to my room. My dad took one suitcase, and I took the other one, and we walked upstairs to my room. There were two closets, so I chose one of them, unpacked, and put everything away. I didn't even use half of the space in the closet or the drawers. After unpacking and checking out the room, we sat down at the desk and talked.

As my parent and I talked, my roommate Jenny and her whole family walked in. She had several boxes, suitcases, and a computer. We introduced ourselves to each other, and her mother started to help her put her things away.

"These closets are so small. I can't fit everything in," Jenny complained.

"You can leave some in your suitcase for now and figure out where to put them later," her mother told her. That's when I piped up.

"You can use the extra space in my closet," I told Jenny.

"I need to head back home," my dad responded, but I decided to go with them. It was a clever way to break the ice with Jenny. I'm glad I got to know her parents a little because Jenny and I would have many conversations about our parents and lives over the coming year.

My first few days on campus were busy with meetings. As I walked around, I was stunned at how big the campus was and how many people were walking or riding bikes around. I worried that I would get lost just going from one class to another, so I practiced going to all my classes. I got lost a couple times, but when I looked like I didn't know where I was going, other students would stop and ask, "Can I help you find the building you're looking for?" I was impressed and relieved that people seemed friendly and helpful. *Maybe this won't be so scary and confusing as I thought*, I mused.

Along with my acceptance to the university, I had been accepted into the College Achievement Admission Program (CAAP). Having low income, the students in CAAP were supported by the Office of Supportive Services in a multifaceted, holistic retention approach that tried to address the needs of the students as individuals. In CAAP, new students met with students who had been through the program before to help the new students adjust to and manage life at a big university. In addition, the older students were assigned to act as mentors to the new students. The program also sponsored periodic activities with successful graduates to come and talk about their experiences. All this was very encouraging for the other new students and me. It helped me think that I could do this thing called "college."

As a first-generation college student, I appreciated parts of the CAAP. Having someone who knows how it feels to be a first-generation college student makes you feel more acclimated. With their encouragement, I got serious about academics. Participating in CAAP is how I got introduced to Michigan State. Initially, I thought, *I don't know why I'm participating in the program. I don't see how this is going to help me. I don't know anything about figuring out this college life, and I'm not looking for any more struggles in my life than I already have.* However, I soon realized that the social support it offered was critical in my acclimation to campus life.

Although I could not predict whether I could meet the challenges I faced as a first-generation college student, I certainly understood my chances of succeeding as a minority, a poor female from a dysfunctional biological family who had grown up in my mother's house, foster homes, in relatives' homes and was adopted at the age of fourteen were not very good. I did not anticipate, however, that repeatedly I would struggle academically to the point of being on probation and on the verge of dropping out or getting expelled. In addition, I did not realize that, in college, I would have more money than I had ever had in my life. Unfortunately, I also squandered it away and became burdened with debt. I've learned money management, so I no longer have those problems.

Excited, anxious, and apprehensive, I began my first week at Michigan State, trying to figure out my place in the academic and social environments. I learned that my roommate represented the stark contrasts that differentiated me from most of my classmates and dorm mates. Jenny came from a wealthy Chicago suburb, drove a flashy car, and often talked on the phone to her well-educated, well-connected parents about what courses to take and how to negotiate the Michigan State social scene. Her parents would go through the course catalog, saying, "You must take this course this semester." It was the kind of advice I would *never* get.

Another difference: Jenny yelled at her parents while on the phone together. After she hung up, I said, "Girl, are you crazy? If I ever talked to my mother or adoptive parents like that, they would kill me!" Also, during finals week, Jenny would always get "care" packages from home that were filled with snacks and candy. My parents wouldn't and couldn't do that. In fact, I now realize they didn't even know that other parents were doing that. They didn't know all the things parents of college students would do to stay in touch and support their children.

When Jenny and I were in bed at night, she shared how she grew up, and I told her what growing up was like for me. We had great fun getting to know each other; however, she kept the room messy. I just couldn't stand it because I'm a cleanliness freak.

"Jenny, you can't walk out of here wearing those wrinkled clothes," I would tell her. I had to teach her how to iron. She'd ask questions like, "You're not going to wash your hair this morning, Kim?"

"No, I'm not," I responded. "We don't wash our hair every day!"

Sometimes, I would look at her and say, "You just went to class, and you did not take a shower? That is not cool!" So, we really got to know each other, including the differences and, in some ways, similarities in our backgrounds.

Jenny came from a home with parents who were able to help her navigate a path in terms of what courses to take and what level of achievement they would accept. Those were the kinds of conversations she had with her parents when they talked on the phone. But when I talked with my adoptive parents, it was more a matter of how to survive—

at college and at home. For instance, my adoptive mother called me, and I could tell she was stressed.

"Co-Co, even though you're working and getting financial aid, and I know we don't give you much, but what we do give you means we have less to use to pay our own bills. It's not easy on us, you know." I had one blood brother, a blood sister, and three adoptive siblings they needed to support at home. So even though my adoptive dad worked on the line at that time, they all still had to make sacrifices for me, like not buying the new furniture they needed and not going to the movies for a night out. So, I felt bad, but at the same time, I was working hard, too, to pay my way.

The differences between Jenny's life and mine were huge. Jenny would talk about family and friends, going overseas to study, and going on great trips for spring break. My spring break was going home to Flint. Summers were for going to summer school and working. It wasn't about exotic travels and all these wonderful things that were going on in her life. But we also bonded when I discovered that Jenny dealt with some unfortunate things in her life that I hadn't experienced.

"When I was twelve, my mother was diagnosed with breast cancer and had to have surgery," Jenny confided. "I was so worried about my mom that instead of going to school, I headed off to the coffee shop and walked around town until it was time to go home. Of course, the school called my parents, and they found out, so I was grounded for a month."

Then a couple of years after, her younger sister was raped by one of the boys in her neighborhood. Her parents didn't report it to the police because they didn't want her sister to have to go to court. Also, they were good friends with the boy's parents, so they didn't want to confront them. I would not have wanted those experiences to happen to me. So, we both had hardships, although our hardships differed from one another's. Talking about these experiences created a bond between us. Still, her whole life was laid out for her by her parents, and I'm thinking, *Oh, girl. This is the good life for you!* In my case, I needed to be independent of my parents, which was my struggle. For me, it was, "I'm here. I have to figure this out on my own." I realized that the only thing my family could tell me was how to become a factory worker. They would have been comfortable had I gone into the Army, where other people would tell me what to do. But, at college, I had to figure it out myself.

One of the first things I learned about Jenny was that she had more money than I had. For instance, she had a beautiful Polo coat. She got in trouble with her parents because she went to the mall and spent $200 on that coat. Her parents argued with her about spending so much money on a coat, but she didn't have to return it. I was like,

"Girl, that coat is bad! My dad doesn't even have a single credit card!" When Dad got his check, we would go to the grocery store, and he would pay the bills with money orders.

Jenny was in a sorority, had this nice car and all these nice clothes. In my junior year, I got a '77 Cutlass my dad paid $300 for. I thought it was the best thing since sliced bread. I was always dodging the people who ticketed cars on campus because I had no money to pay for parking tickets, but I wasn't always successful. Still, I didn't stop parking in places where I knew I would get tickets because it was so much quicker to get to class parking in those places when I was running late.

I developed a diverse group of friends while living in Brody Complex, including a couple of people from a town close to Flint. I felt a special kinship with them because they were from near my hometown. Two other girls who lived across the hall invited me to a party in Bloomfield Hills, an affluent suburb where one of them lived. I accepted the invitation. When I walked into the house, I was amazed at the size and posh furnishings. The living room was full of elegant furniture. The table in the dining room looked like it could fit more than a dozen people. In addition, there was a family room with a big TV, a large kitchen with lots of cabinets and I don't know how many bedrooms were upstairs. I thought, *Oh my God!* It was definitely a culture shock.

My wider group of diverse friends and I had good times in the dorm. It wasn't uncommon for someone to say, "Hey, Kimberly, we're having a party. Do you want to come?"

I realized that as different as we were, we were similar. We were young and experiencing this college adventure together. Even though I had a different story to tell, and they came from more affluent backgrounds, they still had what they called "problems."

Some of them felt bad because their parents were divorced. Some were expected to date a guy studying for a career where he would make lots of money. I thought, *You don't have any problems*, but they thought they did. When I think about this now, I've learned that the kinds of challenges I've had—you don't grow out of them, but you grow stronger as a person as you try to deal with them. You grow, and they manifest themselves in various parts of your life in slightly different forms. For example, I'm still not so good at budgeting and spending money prudently, but I'm better, and I know I need to be responsible.

While confronting the culture shocks of a huge, diverse campus, one of my initial challenges was finding a job. Because my financial aid package included work-study, I was quickly engrossed in a campus job search. The first job I got was in the cafeteria in Brody complex—one of many jobs I had throughout my undergraduate years. I also worked at the post office, the Service Merchandise call center, a housekeeping job for a lady I met over the phone while working at Service Merchandise, plus Burger King, Taco Bell and in telemarketing. Also, I took out loans. Although I had no one to help me figure out which loans I was qualified for and what I had to do to file for financial aid, I figured it out myself and borrowed a lot of money all the way through my undergraduate years and into my graduate program. In addition to the loan my dad took out, my adoptive mother got a loan for about $20,000. This loan was eventually forgiven when she passed away. I also got a Target Teacher Scholarship for $500. There was even a loan forgiveness program if you worked in a Title-I school for five years, which I did. Everything helped.

It took me a while to find my place on campus. But overall, I never felt like I didn't belong at the university or with the friends I made. For a while, it was extremely hard—even intimidating. Just the discipline needed to find my academic and social place was overwhelming. I was like a fish out of water trying to find a place to catch my breath. Often, that place was right back in the safety of my dorm room.

After the first semester, when Jenny came back, her GPA was over 3.0. I had a 0.6! I realized I didn't have the study skills that were required. I didn't have the discipline to concentrate on reading and writing papers repeatedly to make them better. I soon learned how important it was to stay focused on my coursework and be academically prepared. It was really eye-opening because I put in a lot of effort academically in high school. I didn't goof off a lot, and my grades were acceptable. In college, I had to work so much harder than I had imagined if I expected to pass.

As huge as it was, I realize now that I could not have been in a better place than Michigan State. I don't regret any of the setbacks or challenges I've had because all of those things taught me how to be successful. Other things helped me be disciplined, like work-study, for example. My parents said, "Look, girl. This is what's going to keep you in school. You have financial aid; you have work-study." Even though I did my share of partying and drinking, there were many nights when I couldn't do that because I had to go to work. While some students would have chosen not to go to work and go to a party instead, I knew I had to work. I was one of those students who had to work hard for everything I earned despite being in a stable family for once in my life.

Other aspects of my family life were still challenging. For instance, one day, my older brother and his girlfriend were arguing. They went outside; she got his gun from the house and shot him in the stomach and leg. He was hospitalized, and I had to return to MSU and concentrate on school while being scared that my big brother, my hero would die, but he survived.

My adoptive family struggled financially because Dad got hurt in the shop and eventually had to retire due to his shoulder injuries. If he wasn't injured, believe me, he would have continued to work. Two of my adoptive sisters were pregnant, and my adoptive mom was sick with diabetes. Dad took care of it. I have no idea how he could continue to help other people, but he did. He was a funny man who taught me about tolerance and acceptance. No one was a stranger to him. He taught me the spirit of giving. Anyone who knew my dad knows he was a giving man almost to a fault. It was one of his values.

In my sophomore year, I did not get all of my financial aid money. My parents had to produce what I needed. My adoptive mom said, "Co-Co, you will have to come home from the university and attend community college because we don't have the money to support you at Michigan State."

"No, she is going back," Dad interjected. He took out a loan that I didn't know about until years later when my adoptive mom told me. He never once mentioned it to me.

Since I was overwhelmed with academic and personal problems, my undergraduate years were not stellar. While working, I even got into a verbal fight with an athlete in the middle of the Brody cafeteria. He was dating a friend of mine. Over time, my friend and her boyfriend had been having some disagreements and were not getting along.

"You shouldn't be dating him. He is hurting you," I told my friend. "He doesn't really care about you, and he is just using you. You should leave him." Then, I argued with her boyfriend about their relationship. Initially, we started arguing over the phone. We went back and forth about what he was doing that I said disrespected my friend.

"I don't like your attitude toward my friend," I told him. "You treat her like all your other girls! Leave her alone!"

Later, both he and I happened to be in the Brody cafeteria while working. He came up to me and said, "Stay out of our business!" I felt very threatened, so I picked up the closest thing I could find to fight back—a metal fork—and chased him around, yelling, "I'm telling you, stay away from my friend!" Thank God I didn't get out of control! Somebody came and grabbed me, grabbed the fork from my hand and took me away. It is good somebody intervened because he was bigger and taller than I was!

I didn't expect anyone would come up and say anything disrespectful to my face, but he did.

"You bitch! Mind your own business!" he yelled. He probably thought he would scare me or run me off, but I'm not one to back down. That's how I was raised. If somebody gets in your face and starts something, you don't let yourself be pushed around. So, he never talked to me again, nor did I ever say anything to him. In fact, we never saw each other again. My girlfriend split up with him, and he never called or came to the dorm again.

As a result of our fight, I had to go before the Student Review Board.

I don't know what happened to him, whether he was disciplined, but I know I was. I was scared because I could have been kicked out of the university for this. There were students on the board, too. The board put me on probation and kicked me out of Brody. That's how I ended up at another dorm—Yackley-Gilcrest. After the review, I met with the student review board director privately. He really hit home.

"You need to understand that you are at a well-known university, an institution of higher learning. When you fight like you did, you demean yourself and our university. Your behavior was extremely aggressive—not the way we would expect a student to behave, even if you were angry. It just perpetuates stereotypes that white people have of African Americans being belligerent. On top of that, you were in a cafeteria where people were having a meal and trying to relax." He asked if I wanted to graduate from this university.

"Yes!" I exclaimed.

"Well then, you're going about things the wrong way, behaving the way you're behaving," he responded. At first, I was going to say something, but I didn't want to argue because I was scared of getting kicked out of the university. It all happened so fast that it never occurred to me that little spats over the phone would lead up to me chasing a big athlete around the cafeteria with a fork! I was sent to a counseling program. I had to attend meetings with other students who had problems with aggressive behavior. We talked about our own situations, including aggressive incidents we had observed or experienced. We thought of ways each of us might respond differently when confronted by something that could trigger our aggression. At the time, I thought the counseling was not extremely helpful because I didn't think of myself as a physically aggressive person. I kept my mouth shut so I would not get kicked out of the session and probably college. Then, right after the first session, I took a bus home to get away from campus for a couple of days. Coach Kathy picked me up and took me to my adoptive parents' house, where I could calm down and reflect on my actions and their consequences.

Even though I'd felt the need to physically fight for my acceptance and dignity, I eventually realized that if I wanted to graduate, I needed to manage my emotional and academic problems more intentionally and wisely. Unfortunately, as a child, no one ever helped me to understand how to do this.

When I was growing up, people told me, "No, you can't do that!" But they did not help me to understand *why*. My mother and siblings were too focused on themselves to pay much attention to me. Even in my foster homes before we went to The Jacksons, no adult had ever reprimanded me very much. Looking back, it seems to me they were more interested in getting the subsidy money for having foster kids instead of trying to help us learn how to behave properly.

Once again, I felt the need to focus on my studies. I needed at least a 2.0-grade point average to even apply for admission to the university's teacher preparation program. Acceptance into that program also required several interviews, an essay, and recommendations. That's when I realized that my life for the rest of my college years had to have purpose and focus if I really intended to become an educator.

When I returned to campus, I found a different culture at Yackley-Gilcrest. As it turned out, the transfer to Yackley-Gilcrest was good for me. I was with a bunch of girls who were different from my friends at Brody. At Yackley-Gilcrest, we got together and studied. It was actually a mixture of partying and studying, which was enjoyable. I have a picture of my girlfriends and me studying on the lawn. My Brody friends would come over and visit.

"Kim, things are quiet over here," my Brody friends teased.

"Yeah, we're studying and it's a good thing!" I responded.

I stayed until the end of the year and then moved off campus to live with a girlfriend. That was the end of my sophomore year and I never got in trouble for personal behavior again.

Thinking back over this part of my life, I see now how my behavior reflected the harshness of the family models that I grew up with. Although that wasn't true of my adoptive family, the fourteen years that I spent moving from my mother's house to my aunt's house or foster homes left me wanting to protect myself and others, even when it was not helpful to them or even my responsibility. Trying to hustle and take care of myself, dealing with trouble in my foster families, and experiencing conflict with my adoptive mother all foreshadowed the aggressive behavior that came out when I got to college.

When I was growing up, I wanted new things—especially new clothes; I got them while in college. They were mostly things my roommates had already. I got them because I spent my scholarship funds, loan, and work money on things I never had. I spent a lot of time shopping. During my freshman and sophomore years, I wished I had a car on campus. When my dad bought me that old Cutlass during my junior year, I got so many parking tickets that he had to take out a loan to pay them off, or I wouldn't have graduated.

I did accomplish one wish that was uppermost in my thinking. When I was a sophomore, I went to court and changed my adoptive last name to my birth name—Leverette. However, other wishes remained unfulfilled: to know and learn about my biological father, hear my mother say, "I love you," and generally, just to be loved. These wishes were more difficult to fulfill because they were basically out of my control.

Chapter 4

THE WILL TO SURVIVE

A cademically at Michigan State University, my story was not only just as grim as my social and financial stories; it also lasted longer. I was on academic probation; it seemed like forever. Now, I tell people, "Once you get into a hole academically, it's hard to get out and raise that grade point average. So, monitor your grades from the start and don't get into a hole like I did. A 1.5 or 1.0—that is not going to make it. If you fail your classes, you get a 0.0—that will not get it!"

I repeated a lot of coursework. My first year in the fall of 1989 got off to a terrible start. I took an American Thought and Literature preparatory writing skills class and got a "pass." In Quantitative Techniques, my grade was 1.0. I had Music 135 (Music in Education), a required course for students in elementary education, and failed. I took Natural Science and got a 1.0. My GPA during that first semester at Michigan State was 0.6. I thought, *It's over for me!* But I was allowed to continue on academic probation.

I took the second part of Elements in Writing in the winter quarter and got a 2.5. I had another developmental writing class and received a 2.5. But in the Individual, Marriage and Family course, my grade was 1.5. What I knew about marriage and family definitely did not match their expectations! In Elements of Algebra, I got a 1.0. At least my GPA went from 0.6 to 1.3, which allowed staying another quarter.

In the spring quarter of my freshman year, I had to enroll in the music class again, where the focus of this class was on playing different instruments. Maybe even more than in mathematics, I had no notion of music. "I always listened to music as I grew up, but how could I get through this class with no resources to play instruments?" I asked myself. When I was young, I thought, *Maybe I should learn to play the violin or any instrument.* It was not anything I needed or could afford to do. In elementary school, I was a member of the school choir. I soon discovered that singing was not my forte. With so little exposure to or musical talent, is it any wonder that I did not do well in the required music course? As I began the course for the second time, instead of offering to mentor me or suggesting people who could mentor me, the professor told me, "Kimberly, you will fail this course again. You should just drop out of Michigan State University entirely. You're not making the grade." I was infuriated! I set myself to pass the course, even if just barely, but then decided the best avenue was to drop it.

Part of the reason I stuck it out at college was because every time I went home, Dad bragged about me to anyone and everyone who would listen to him. He was a huge fan of Michigan State sports, so the idea that I was a first-generation college student in such a place was phenomenal for him. But my grades were miserable. I told Dad I was not doing well.

"Baby, you are going to make it. You are just as smart as the rest of those people. Just keep going." And he was right. When I started, neither my parents nor I had any idea of what it took to stay in college. They just knew I was there, and I can't even begin to tell you how proud my dad was of me!

Teaching was my goal when I started at Michigan State. I wanted to be a teacher, and I declared teacher education as my major. At one point, I considered communication arts a major, and I did a lot of coursework in that area. However, I ended up really enjoying the field experience that we did in the teacher preparation program. With assigned work in a K-12 school, the first course was designed as an exploratory course to find out what teaching is like. It was a great class for foundational stuff, and I thought it was a wonderful opportunity when they had us go into an actual classroom and do observations. The field experience helped me start seeing the classroom from "the other side of the desk."

During sophomore year, I had the opportunity to volunteer with students in East Lansing, where the university was located. It felt good. It felt right! I couldn't have chosen a better field for myself. I found that I could have an impact on students' lives. That was especially important to me. I had to get my grades up to get a GPA that met the requirement for acceptance into the teacher preparation program. This meant having to repeat some classes. I still had my grade school report card to remind me that I was a kid in the gray area—actually more like in a black hole because I didn't excel in any particular subject. It felt like I had encountered every obstacle and every roadblock, but I didn't want to be a failure. The person I most didn't want to let down was *me*. As I got closer to graduation, I also realized how my experience could really impact my family and my community. It would be so impressive to have a college graduate in my family. I just wanted to be able to go home and say, "I have a bachelor's degree from Michigan State University." That was really important to me.

To stay on track academically, I went to summer school most summers. There were times, in the first two years, when I thought I'd better go home and try community college because I wasn't doing well in so many courses. Nevertheless, I hung in there. I realized I needed to develop study skills, including creating a schedule that would keep me organized and use my time efficiently. I bought a special notebook that had times by the hour from 8:00 a.m. to 12:00 p.m.

I wrote in my class times, work times, and then study times in what was left over. Sometimes, I met with a classmate or a small study group to study for an exam. That was helpful because I could find out how other students understood the course material. My freshman roommate, Jenny, also helped by setting an example for me—reading and studying for several hours every day. I hung in there and finally ended up in the College of Education after spending an extra year plus summer school to take needed classes and meet the GPA requirement.

To me, college was about surviving. I thought about my birth mom and brothers and sisters, who didn't have the support I had from my track coach and adoptive parents to push me to college. Survival was on my mind in high school and throughout college. When I started college, I knew I wanted to get a college degree, but what about that music class and poetry class that gave me trouble? Fortunately, they changed the requirement for the music course to an option, so I didn't have to take it after all. I found another course to substitute for the poetry one and passed that class.

My wish to change my adopted last name back to my birth name finally came true. When I was a sophomore, I got some money together, went to the courthouse in East Lansing, and had my name legally changed back to Leverette. My dad understood how much it meant to me to have my birth name.

"Co-Co," he said, "I know you love your birth mom very much. You treasure your birth name because it connects you with her in a concrete and obvious way. It is part of your identity. I can accept that and admire your determination to make that change." The change, however, caused huge problems between my adoptive mother and me.

"I don't understand. What's wrong with Jackson as your last name? If you change it, it's like we're not your parents anymore." We always had our differences because I've always felt very strongly that I had my own voice and could speak up and stand up for myself. I knew what I wanted, whether it was right or wrong. Stubborn as I was—stubborn and defiant, not a rule follower—I was able to figure some things out. For instance, I knew that I had legal authority to do whatever I wanted about my name since I was over eighteen.

I was determined to get a college degree despite all the pitfalls I experienced. It didn't help seeing other African American students drop out. They were kids from all over the state, all over the country. I thought, *You guys are so* smart. *Why are you quitting? What the heck is really going on?* I started seeing people I thought were really smart go home and not return. That was scary. I kept thinking, *These kids are so smart; they have everything ahead of them.*

I wonder how many of these kids, just in the Brody Complex alone, stay and how many go home? They seem so much smarter than me, but they're going home. That was unnerving. What did they do or didn't do that made them go home? Hard work can uncover talent, but talent requires hard work. That part was intimidating.

When I started my junior year, the university changed from quarters to semesters.

The College of Education also began a five-year teacher preparation program to replace the traditional four-year one. A woman in the advisement office in the college met with me. She asked me to interview for the Multiple Perspectives program, which had an urban focus. I told the advisor, "I'm not interested in an urban program. I went to urban schools all my life, and I want to experience something different." Nevertheless, I met with the professor who directed the program to find out what the program was about.

"I want to be clear," I told the director, "I am not interested in urban teaching."

"You don't have to be in this program," the professor responded. "The advisement office makes decisions about what programs entering students might be interested in and sets them up for interviews with the program. You can just go back to the advisement office and tell them what program you want to interview with. You might want to come along with other students joining the MP group on a trip to the Flint Community Schools to hear the superintendent talk about the district and the value of Michigan State working with the district."

Curious and somewhat intrigued, I went on the trip. The superintendent's talk about the need for outstanding teachers in the district impressed me. Not only did I know the district from a student's point of view, but I also felt a great desire to be part of helping the district by educating kids like me. At the end of the talk, I looked over at the professor who accompanied us and nodded. I was going to join the teacher education program.

Following graduation from the undergraduate program, the program's fifth year was a year-long school internship with a couple of master's level courses each semester. To get my teaching certificate from the state, I had to complete that internship year and the state's certification tests.

I went through the undergraduate ceremony at the end of the spring semester of 1994, even though I had twelve credits remaining to finish. When I was ready to graduate, the university put a hold on my account. I had over $1000 in parking tickets that had to be paid!

"Co-Co, how did this happen? Where did you park? Didn't you know you owed so much?" Dad asked. Again, he ended up paying the money so I could graduate. I enrolled in summer school, finished those twelve credits, and officially received my much-anticipated bachelor's degree. Finally, I was ready for my internship to begin in the fall of 1994.

For my internship, I was placed at Brownell Elementary school. I was excited about this placement because the teachers and parents knew me. Plus, I would be close to my family and stay with them if I needed to. Plus, my boyfriend was there. I also knew I'd be accepted in any of the schools since I'd attended so many of them. That would make it easier for me to adjust to my new role as a full-time teacher intern.

The internship program at Michigan State was not easy. I complained a lot during my internship about how hard it was. For instance, I had to create a concept map for what I would teach over the course of a semester. This was extremely demanding work for me and took a lot of time. After completing my first map, I changed my view of a concept map from just a required assignment that didn't seem helpful to a useful tool for understanding what my students were supposed to learn and what I would be responsible for teaching. My initial concerns weren't so different from those of other interns. Almost all of us thought our first attempts at identifying what our students should learn and integrating multiple subject matter areas to make it more meaningful was tough work. However, after we all got through our initial resistance and pushed our thinking, we found that we could use our concept maps as an instructional tool to illustrate how the subject matter fit together. We talked about how the concept maps helped us connect what students said about what they were learning. We were usually able to link it to our concept map. Those concept maps became a driving force in the classroom. It also limited behavior problems because the students owned what they were learning, so they paid attention.

Once again, I ran out of money. I could not pay my rent, tuition, or the test fee to retake the mathematics portion of the required state exam for teacher certification. I had failed it on all my earlier attempts. I was convinced that I would have to drop out for lack of money to carry me through the next and final semester of my quest for teacher certification.

Since I didn't believe I could pass the math portion of the state exam and go on with my internship in January, I just stopped showing up for the class after Thanksgiving. I hid out for about a week and didn't know my next step. I thought, *I'm in trouble. I'm in this relationship with a guy I've known since high school, and we were breaking up. I'm in this program that requires mathematics understanding that I don't have. I'm in my sixth year in college, and I can't do this!* So, I stayed home and sat on the couch. I left a message on the phone saying, "I'm not here. If you want, you can leave a message for me." I didn't want anyone to find me.

When two of the teacher education professors who worked with me for three years found out that I was not at my placement, they started asking questions at the school about why I wasn't there. They called a couple times, but I chose to ignore their calls because I didn't want to talk about my problems. I was sure they would not understand what I was going through. I felt so inadequate. I would hear the other interns say, "Oh, that test was so easy," and I thought *it wasn't easy at all.*

I had so many gaps in my learning. But that wasn't actually what I was thinking about. I was thinking about each time I took the math test. I was thinking, *You are not going to be able to do this because you are not smart enough to do it.* I just kept thinking that. I already had a bachelor's degree, so I just went back to my apartment and started thinking about what I could do with a bachelor's degree besides teaching. Then, I heard a knock on the door. It was my professors! They asked if they could come in and talk to me.

I didn't have a dime in the bank, a dime in my pocket, a dime in my purse, or anywhere else. I was really taken aback when those professors said they would help me pay for tuition, rent, and the test fee. Over the three years that I've known them, I had learned that one of the professors was somebody you did not say "no" to.

"Staying away from your school placement and your classes is not helpful," she said. "I want you to go back to your school tomorrow, and I'll see you in class on Thursday."

"Okay, okay," I relented. She believed in me. She could say to me, "Fly a rocket up into space today and be back in time for lunch tomorrow," and somehow, I'd do it! They didn't make a big deal about my trouble passing that math test. They still believed in me for some reason, even when I didn't. I don't know how they did it. They convinced me to go back to the school where I was doing my internship and finish the semester. I was surprised and overwhelmed—not only by their kindness and compassion—but also by their faith in me that I was worth the investment. They taught me a valuable lesson: All it takes is for one caring adult to believe in you. They stand in the trenches with young people, remove barriers, provide coaching and intervention where needed, and become part of the journey and celebration of life for you!

At that time, I lived in an apartment with my boyfriend, who I had dated throughout my years at Michigan State. We were going through a lot. He was my high school boyfriend; in fact, we had been engaged. However, I broke it off when he went into the service and when I started college. He was in the service for a couple of years, but he went AWOL. We had started seeing each other again and decided to live together, but the relationship was not good.

One night, we got into a bad confrontation, yelling and pushing each other.

"You bastard!" I shouted. "Don't put your hands on me! Stay away from me!"

"I'll show you what you deserve!" He yelled and banged me against the wall. The neighbors called the police. When the police came, they saw Calvin's picture in his uniform on the bookshelf. The officer in charge said, "Oh, you're in the military." My heart sank since we both knew he was AWOL.

He went to court. He had a horrible life growing up—much worse than mine in many ways. I wrote the judge, asking the judge to be lenient and not sentence him for an extended time, even though he was AWOL for almost a year and then dishonorably discharged. Surprisingly, the judge did go light on him. He was in jail for ninety days. The judge said that she wanted to help because of the letter from this young lady who said he was going through some tough times. Yes, he had had a tough life, and I decided to support him. I just did not want to see a lengthy prison term for him.

After that tumultuous fall internship semester, I broke up with Calvin for good. I went home to live with my adoptive parents. Unfortunately, I had to wait a year before I could do the spring semester internship because I still had not passed the state mathematics exam. In the interim, I taught as a substitute teacher in the Flint Community Schools, which gave me an income and more experience and exposure as a teacher in the Flint school system.

Having finally passed the mathematics exam in the fall of 1995, I finished my internship in the spring of 1996 and got my teacher certification. Finally, I was ready for a career that would change my life and the lives of the children and adults with whom I worked.

Once my college experience was over, I thought back to when I first went to Michigan State. I felt overwhelmed by the number of students and the vastness of the campus. If a person like me could figure that all out, successfully navigate that situation and come back from a 0.6 GPA, I think that's rather good. I'm not the most intelligent person in the room, but I am pretty tenacious, and I have that "stick-with-it-ness." I had thought you had to be a really smart person to go to college. Well, it turns out that there are other characteristics you must have that I guess many people don't have, but I do. I thought to myself, *I'm determined, and my toughness helps me stay the course. I didn't give up on a dream I never thought I would have in the first place. I'm so glad I haven't disappointed Dad. He believes in me so much, and I'm glad I exceeded his expectations for me.*

Having received my teacher certification, I decided to apply for a position in the Flint Community Schools since both my birth and adoptive families were there. I accepted a fourth-fifth grade teaching position at Doyle-Ryder Elementary School, beginning my teaching career and eventually administration in the place I knew best. Now, I was ready to add to my wish list. My new wish was to be a great educator and help urban kids succeed.

Chapter 5

A CALL TO TEACH

I knew the Flint District well. I had attended Flint schools growing up and went on to do my internship in two Flint elementary schools. I had gained experience by doing a lot of substitute teaching during the two semesters I waited to pass the state mathematics test for teacher certification. Knowing influential people in the district and being a strong teacher candidate, I wasn't surprised that I was hired for my first teaching position beginning in the fall of 1996.

As I got into my teaching, in my head and heart, I knew for sure that teaching was my purpose in life. Because of the yearlong internship and my year of substitute teaching, I was assigned to a split fourth and fifth-grade class with twenty-eight students at Doyle-Ryder Elementary School. My class included about seven special-needs students who integrated into my classroom. This meant I got to work closely with the special education teacher. There were so many students with lives like mine that it was easy to connect to them. I fell in love with all of them—every last one of them. I just loved them so much because I saw so much of me in all of the children. That pushed me harder to teach them well. I didn't let their life stories set my expectations for what they could achieve. My expectations were exceedingly high. I was very loving to my students. I was concerned, and they knew that I cared. For instance, when I had playground duty, I would jump rope with the girls doing Double Dutch and referee the basketball game the boys organized.

There were a lot of smart kids in my class who could have been overlooked by a teacher who hadn't had the kind of childhood I had. Helen was one of my students with whom I made a strong connection. Helen lived in the Wiley Home for Children, an orphanage after her mother was found murdered on the streets of Flint. I just fell in love with Helen. However, she had a lot of problems. One time she was bothering other students.

"Helen, you come up here and sit by me so I can keep an eye on you," I said. She proceeded to steal several items out of my desk. I had no idea that she took these things until her social worker brought her back to the school one afternoon, along with all these supplies from my desk.

"Did you realize Helen stole all this stuff from your desk?" The social worker asked.

"I think she needs to be punished by putting her in school detention."

"I want to have a talk with Helen," I responded. I walked over to Helen and bent down, looking directly at her. "I'm disappointed. I love you. I'd give you anything I have. I can't believe you stole out of my desk." She was very remorseful. She cried and apologized.

That was when Helen was in the fourth grade. I kept her all the way through fifth grade. I had other problems with her, but she never stole from me again. The social worker told me that her mother had been a prostitute. She would have sex with men in hotels while her kids hid in the closets. While the men were distracted, the kids would crawl out of the closet and take money out of the men's pants pockets. I concluded that her stealing was a learned behavior.

I had another student named Lenny. His grandfather killed his grandmother, and his father killed his mother. Can you imagine the anger he felt? He was the cutest kid with the biggest smile. He was loving, but he was angry—terribly angry. I tried to look into the students' feelings, backgrounds, and what they had gone through. I would say to each of them, "In this classroom, you're safe. In this classroom, you matter, and in this classroom, you're important. You can come to this classroom and show me how smart you are."

We did just that. I'm not saying I didn't have behavior problems, but I found that listening to the students during our "Morning Meeting," which was a time to talk about the day ahead, helped provide a way of taking care of their personal needs. For instance, one student told us, "My mom had a baby last night, so now I have a sister."

"My dad took me bowling last night and we had ice cream after," another student shared.

"My dad hit my mom last night, and she cried, and he left," another confessed.

We'd all listen and ask questions or just comment. We had a class that was inclusive of everyone. Each child had a voice in what we did. Everyone helped with the organization of the day, like whether they needed time to finish their silent reading or whose turn it was to feed the fish. The result was that their acceptance of personal responsibility increased along with their academic skills. They needed a teacher to listen to them. As it turned out, I needed them, too. I drew so much strength and wisdom from those kids. When I listened to the kids, I found that I could see things from their perspectives. I also saw that what I had learned in my teacher preparation program worked when I applied it in my classroom. Even Lenny let go of a little bit of his anger.

During my first year of teaching, I found myself walking out the school door, crying like a baby several times a week because of what the children needed. I constantly wondered if I was doing all that I could. Right away, I noticed that several teachers were not using the student data provided by the student's previous teachers. Some of my colleagues never looked at it. Some reviewed it after three or four weeks of working with the students, and some of us reviewed it before the students came to school. It bothered me that many teachers did not look at their students' files before school started.

The semester before I finished my internship, I taught full-time as a substitute teacher. The teacher's lesson plans that I was supposed to follow focused on an activity or pages in textbooks or workbooks. The plans didn't tell me what knowledge or skills were essential for the class to learn, let alone the students individually. I felt like I was wasting the students' time and mine when I didn't know something about the students and which assignments and activities would help them learn.

In the second year as a certified teacher, I had one of those classrooms where the principal placed children with problems and special needs. I had a couple dyslectic kids. One had attention deficit hyperactivity disorder (ADHD) and couldn't sit still for more than a few minutes. One child was so quiet and sullen that I worried she might've been molested at home. At the time, I didn't know why the principal put so many of these kids in my room. I thought maybe it was because I was young and naïve, but I didn't care.

As the year progressed, the principal and other teachers would ask, "How do you do this? How do you connect with those kids and their lives so quickly?"

"I think I need to establish personal, trusting relationships with my students before I can teach them anything," I responded. "I know the children need to feel they are important to the group and me. I know how to help them understand that they have a role in the classroom. For example, one thing we do is celebrate each kid's birthday. I know that is special because it was something I never experienced as a child, and I wished I had. When I give this kind of attention to each child, it shows them that I care about them as individuals and expect them to show how smart they really are."

I had students who were siblings. Actually, I had two sets of siblings. They brought so many different and difficult dynamics into the classroom due to the things going on in their lives. Because of my background and experiences, I didn't have to figure that all out because I was pretty much an expert in sibling relationships. I knew and understood what was going on with them, such as when they were tired, needed attention, or hungry. It was like I just inherently knew what to do with those children. They didn't scare me because my siblings and I went through the same experiences in my family. We took care of each other since our mother was incapable of taking charge and caring for us.

People would come into my classroom and say, "Where did you come from? What school did you attend? How do you know about cooperative learning?" In the Michigan State University Teacher Preparation Program, we participated in conferences with parents, and Individualized Education Plan (IEP) meetings to discuss and plan for special education student learning. In addition, we participated in staff meetings and in all kinds of discussions during my internship. I just knew I was well prepared to do this job. At the time, even though I still considered myself a novice, I had a particular skill set and knowledge that I gained from my experience at Michigan State. It made for confidence. People were actually asking, "How did you know this?"

"I learned it at Michigan State."

"Wow! Can we get more teachers like you?" was their response. I didn't even think there was anything strange about people saying this.

There's a broad knowledge gap between a semester of student teaching and a yearlong internship and having the kinds of experiences we had. Even in my first year of teaching, my colleagues came to me for advice, although they had been teaching much longer than I had.

"How do you know how to put the children in the learning centers and have them not talk about things that are not related?" They would ask.

"I learned about centers in my teacher preparation program and worked in several schools where teachers used them, so I got first-hand experience."

On the other hand, when I first started teaching, I thought, *I'm never going back to Michigan State. Those people are crazy because of their high expectations for my performance and the amount of work required.* However, the more I continued to learn from teaching, the more I appreciated my experiences at Michigan State. Still, I was tired. I had been through a lot. It was a tough program, and I had my own personal issues to resolve. After six years of struggling through it all, I was ready to be done with studying. The intensity with which we worked, the high expectations and the critical feedback had been a lot to deal with, especially after such a tumultuous childhood, changing grade schools every year. The college professors didn't just say, "Good job." They had long conversations with me, and they continued to push and push.

"Why did you plan that activity for your lesson? How does it fit with what you know about your students? Tell me about one of your students and why this will help them learn. How will you know that student learned what you're trying to teach?" These were the questions I was asked. At the time, it drove me crazy, but as I started teaching, I understood that it was just a phenomenal program. Now, I sit back and sing praises for the program. I will always feel that my experience was the best that I could ever had.

After my second year of teaching, I was approached by the school principal to teach in the gifted program. I told them I didn't want to do that, but I was willing to attend the summer conference. I was nervous because the students were not children from backgrounds similar to mine. The Challenge Program, as the gifted program was called, had children of well-educated parents—judges, lawyers, doctors and such. It was housed in Doyle-Ryder, where I taught in the "Neighborhood Program" section of the building. I was keenly aware of the segregation between these two programs housed in the same school and how their opportunities were quite different.

The Challenge Program's teachers wanted me to teach with them in the gifted program. I didn't want to do it. The school principal told me to go through the training, which I did. Then, I met with all the gifted program teachers. I came back and spoke with the principal.

"I need to talk with you," I said. "We have some gifted kids in the Neighborhood Program. I think that every last one of the kids in the school is gifted, just in a unique way. I know they call it the 'Neighborhood Program,' but I have a gifted program in my classroom, and I would like to continue to work with my students. So, if you think I'm a gifted teacher and have all these skills (which I didn't think I had at that time), then I want to use them in the Neighborhood Program. I want to stay in that program."

"You know what, Kimberly? Okay," the principal smiled at me and agreed. I was really happy about that.

Another iron in the fire that came up during my second year of teaching was the offer of another outstanding position. Mr. Cleary, the Title I Program's reading teacher, told me he planned to retire. (Title I provides federal assistance to schools with high percentages of low-income families to help ensure all children meet challenging state academic standards.) He was my former eighth-grade middle school teacher. He would come into my classroom and watch me while I taught reading. Because he recognized my ability to connect with my students and get them productively involved in reading, he approached me.

"You know what? Would you be interested in my Title I support job? I think you would do an excellent job. You would have an opportunity to use your skills to work not just with kids in your classroom, but with kids all over the school."

Although I hadn't thought about aspiring to that position, Mr. Cleary encouraged me. He said, "I'm retiring next year, and I'm going to recommend you for my job." A bit surprised and apprehensive, I thought, *What? That is one of those coveted positions that senior-level staff feel they deserve.* I imagined the senior teachers would proclaim, "That position should be mine. I've been here a long time, so naturally, I should get the job."

Helping kids learn to read through the Title I program meant that I could concentrate on working with children who needed close attention. I would be someone who could focus solely on their learning to read. This was my strongest teaching area, and I thought I could make a difference for these children. I remembered how I received help throughout the Title I math program to learn what I needed to pass sixth-grade math. I have always been thankful for that teacher who worked so closely with me to help me pass. Now, I had the opportunity to help children in the same manner. Because I would be in charge of the program at Doyle-Ryder, the job was also a steppingstone to taking some administrative responsibility, which was my ultimate career goal.

When the teachers came back in the fall of my third year at Doyle-Ryder, the principal announced that I was the Title I reading teacher. I had accepted the job over the summer and, as I predicted, I got a lot of opposition for it. Some teachers confronted me.

"How do you think you can handle this? You're just a third-year teacher!" One teacher said.

The principal reassured me by saying, "Kimberly, you just get in there and do your job. Do what I asked you to do and what Mr. Cleary assured me you are capable of doing."

Characteristically, I began the reading program with a lot of determination, grit, and a plan of action. I had to establish my credibility quickly. The teachers were not happy about it at all, but I told them, "Okay, let me show you why I do what I do. This year, students are expected to read twenty-five books in a given amount of time. The amount of time depends on the individual's reading level when we start this project. I will adjust the numbers as the students get interested and begin reading at levels beyond where they started." It wasn't just the Title I Neighborhood Program students affected by this decision. The entire school got involved.

I recognized it was a lot of fun teaching kids reading skills and equipping them with the vocabulary. The comprehension was phenomenal. I never stopped getting the opposition from some teachers in particular, but they sort of backed off. My second year in that position wasn't as bad as the first. The work I was doing paid off in exceptional results for the students. The changes I saw were enough for me and should have been enough for the skeptical teachers. It wasn't my intention to compete with the other teachers. Still, I was thankful I had this job because the students made significant progress with their reading. The teachers were both surprised and pleased to see this.

People in the central district office recognized my teaching ability. They would call me and say, "We're having a discussion and we want you to be in on it." Flattered to be invited to participate in the district's literacy planning, I felt recognized for my hard work and its results.

As if my plate wasn't already full of my teaching responsibilities, I realized that to achieve my goal to work in school or district administration, I needed a master's degree. I was determined not to return to Michigan State since I had such a challenging time in my undergraduate years there. Instead, I investigated other master's programs within a reasonable driving distance of Flint. I asked a professor who had helped me finish my bachelor's degree to write me a letter of recommendation for the University of Michigan Flint. The professor told me that since I had already paid for so many credits towards a master's degree from Michigan State, by taking the internship courses, I should take the degree at Michigan State. My thought was, "Well, I don't care how many credits I have. I'm not going back to Michigan State because it's too hard."

"Oh, no, you will go back to Michigan State and get your master's there," the professor said. So, she basically talked me into the difficult classes I was trying to avoid and that forty-minute commute for another year and a half. I worked full-time as a teacher while I drove back and forth to Michigan State in the evening for classes since there were no online courses that I could take. It was tiring. In 2000, I got a master's degree in Curriculum and Instruction from Michigan State. In the long run, I didn't regret the decision.

In the master's program, I made new friends. One night during a class break, one of them, a woman named Mary from California, talked about an upcoming study abroad experience she had enrolled in. My attention perked up. Michigan State offered master's level summer courses at several locations around the world as a means of attracting and servicing teachers in international schools, as well as providing an international experience for students at the main campus. Mary said she was going to the program offered at Valbonne, France.

"I'm going," I said immediately.

"Well, Kim, it's kind of too late," Mary replied. "You know this is a very expensive trip, and you have to have all this paperwork turned in before you go." Since the trip included the last two classes I needed for my master's degree, I responded, "Well, you guys are going; why can't I go?" When

I found out that the others who were going had already made travel plans, and I couldn't get on their flights, I thought, *"Those guys must have travel experience or else it's just for rich kids to participate in. I can't believe I'm going to try to do this!"* It was something I had never even considered possible for me when I was an undergraduate. It reminded me of my freshman roommate and how I thought that traveling abroad was for other kids. They expected it. Not me.

Friends and family told me, "Don't fly by yourself. You'll get lost. You don't speak French; how will you know what to do once you arrive in France?" There had been a recent plane crash, with quite a loss of American lives. I knew my family was worried about my going. I had never traveled abroad, but I said, "Why not?"

I went over to the Office of International Studies, where I got the paperwork. I talked to people there and in the College of Education. I impressed upon them that I really wanted to participate because I had never been out of the country. People in various offices made it happen. They had me running and jumping through all these hoops.

"You need to fill out this paperwork today! Do you have a passport? You have to register for the classes you will take over there."

I got all the paperwork turned in, obtained a passport, packed my bags, and got on that flight to France all by myself. It was a big deal! It was pretty strange because when I was walking down the hall in my dorm in France, Mary stepped out and screamed, "Girl, you are crazy! You have a lot of nerve! You pulled it off!"

"I don't know how, but here I am," I said, laughing hysterically.

The program lasted six weeks. We collaborated and worked in groups, just like we did back on campus. What was incredible was that the students in those groups were from all over the world. I got to know people from Germany, Indonesia, and Japan—people from places that I thought I would never get to see.

We were there for the fourteenth of July, their national Bastille Day holiday. It was pretty cool to participate in the festivities. And then, of course, we went to restaurants where the food was different and better than the places I went to at home—well, better except for my mom's cooking. We were also there at the time of the famous bicycle race, Tour de France. We saw a little bit of it. Our itinerary was constantly changing. Once a week, we had a group excursion organized by the college. We went to places together like the market, and we went shopping. Those were not mandatory, but who wouldn't want to go on an excursion with the group?

I was like, "Okay, where are we going next?" I just took it all in. We went to a perfume factory and got a chance to have some perfume custom made. That was really cool.

When we had a chance to be on our own, Mary kept saying, "I want to go to Paris." But when she and I were making plans for a stop in Paris on our return home, Mary said she didn't have any money.

"Mary, the flight to Paris is short. I have some money," I told her. "We're going to use this money, and you can pay me back when we get to the States, but I am not leaving without going to Paris."

Mary was my guide. She figured out what we were going to do. So, I just packed my travel bags and went along. We went to Paris and saw the Eiffel Tower and the wonderful sights around us. I was in awe. I kept saying to myself, "*I can't believe this is happening. This is so cool! I'm so lucky to be here!*" I was just so incredibly fortunate to be able to have that experience, even though I had to wait until I did my master's program to go.

When I returned to Flint after my summer in France, with my master's degree in hand, I was again the Title I reading teacher, but with a broadened understanding of world places, cultures, and the people who lived in them. Even if my students couldn't have such experiences, I brought my own perceptions and expanded understanding of other people to my work with children. Talking about my experiences and showing pictures helped my students become curious about places beyond Flint and encouraged them to aspire to go to places they may have never even imagined.

In spring 2003, I had a new career opportunity. When the district personnel office called to offer me the Social Studies Instructional Specialist job, I readily accepted it. In that position, I worked with a committee to develop pacing charts for social studies, grades K-12. These gave teachers and administrators information about what children should learn at different points in their education. For example, the charts for third- and fourth-grade social studies contained guidelines on sequencing topics and how long each unit should take to teach. Another part of the job was to offer professional development on the social studies pacing charts and support their implementation in individual buildings. Although I had changed from literacy to social studies, I was already well versed in social studies. It was my teaching minor in my undergraduate program.

This change was both an opportunity to expand my role in the district and a chance to work on a content area I knew well. I found out what really goes on at a district level in this role. For example, I saw central office administrators involved in small group discussions and making decisions that affected everyone in a given program. When those not involved in these discussions found out they were being told they had to change, they found ways to avoid carrying out the "order." I also learned that certain central office administrators were always helping their friends. This resulted in funds going to the same people all of the time. I could change this approach in social studies, but there wasn't much I could do across the board. So, I thought, *If I am ever in a position to make district-wide changes, I will find ways for all teachers to participate, or at least be represented, in the decision-making process.*

Once again, I was eager to continue my education as part of my pursuit of a district-level administrative position. I enjoyed the intellectual stimulation, the collegiality, and the collaboration of studying with like-minded people. Oakland University offered an Educational Specialist program to people with a master's degree. The classes were near Flint, so I didn't have to travel too far. I started that program in 2006. It was exciting to take doctoral-level classes. By taking the Education Specialist classes, I thought that I could get a feel for what the doctoral classes would be like and whether I wanted to apply for the doctoral degree program later. I completed the program in 2008 with a concentration in Educational Leadership.

After the social studies specialist position, I became a literacy coach for the district. Changing central office jobs was not easy. Learning how to work effectively with teachers was just as challenging as it was for me while working on my degree. Having other administrators and teachers to talk with helped a lot. Their experiences gave me much to think about, and they helped me form a new identity as a literacy coach.

As a literacy coach, I worked on developing Writer's Workshops for first through sixth-grade teachers. Writer's Workshop is an approach to teaching writing in a way that helps students draft stories and essays. It also required sharing the writing with classmates to get suggestions for improvements. The students used these suggestions to edit their pieces. I not only provided districtwide professional development on Writer's Workshop teaching methods, but I also successfully implemented the units at two elementary schools and modeled mini lessons in classrooms so that teachers could see this special pedagogy in action.

My individual experiences continued to shape my professional life, not only in my empathy for students growing up in circumstances similar to my own but also in working with my professional colleagues. For example, on one occasion, I went to lunch with other coaches. I will never forget it. We were sitting around the table, and one of the literacy coaches started complaining about her mother. She freely talked about her mother being mentally ill and how she had been in and out of the hospital.

"That's not my mother anymore," the coach announced. I didn't say anything. I sat there like I was frozen. You never know what someone else is going to say. Also, you never know how much words can impact you. I thought, *Wow! Her perspective on her mother and her mental illness is the exact opposite of mine because I would die for my mom. I'd do anything for her.* Everyone doesn't feel the same way about people with mental illness. Because I grew up in that situation, I have empathy. I have a heart for people, and I don't think that anyone should sit around and be a judge of people. I remembered what people said about my mother, things like, "She could have pulled herself together and got her kids out of foster care into a permanent home." Well, guess what? That didn't happen. But I'm never going to give up on loving her because of life's circumstances.

At the end of my second year in the literacy coach position, I was still in pursuit of the Education Specialist degree, and I got another call. Again, it was someone I had worked with at the central office.

"There's a position opening at Pierce Elementary School for an assistant principal. We think you should apply." Pierce was one of the premier schools where the district placed academically successful students. I was still committed to helping disadvantaged children, but this was a chance to get the administrative experience for which I was aiming. I followed his advice and was hired for the job. I worked with Kathy, the principal at Pierce, for two years. I learned that there was more to working with children than just being in the classroom.

Kathy had grand expectations and a reputation for being difficult because she was so demanding; but I learned a lot from her. I saw how she worked for her kids at a different level—inside and outside the classroom and school building. Other people didn't realize what excellent work she was doing at the school and in the neighborhood. I saw her in the cafeteria—one of the best times and places to observe kids hanging out—and I saw how Kathy interacted with the students. She would even take up a broom and sweep the cafeteria floor. I thought, *Wow! She sets an example for all of us to pitch in to take care of our school and be around the students.*

At Pierce, the teaching staff had test scores in their hands even before the principal. They sat down and collaborated on how to respond to the results and planned for the students' continuing education. Those teachers seemed to prefer to take control and work together rather than have administration tell them what to do. They'd plan for what classroom the kids should be in next fall and say, "We're going to move these kids to Mary's room. She'll work with them on their comprehension skills. Let's place some of the kids with lower math scores in June's room and the others in Dan's room because they know how to help kids understand the math." It was the teacher leaders who took control of the decision-making without making any excuses. Even when the student population changed, the teachers' expectations did not. They still had high learning goals for children. It was really powerful, especially when district personnel asked me, "How in the world do you work with Kathy?!" I did it because I could see that she didn't get in the way of the teachers working together and the results were good. It was all part of her plan to get teachers to take control of their students' learning rather than simply follow someone else's dictates.

I was impressed by the collaboration among teachers. They were impressed by my ability to work with a demanding boss. Kathy was not a people person, but we were complementary because she was great with kids. I connected well with both kids and parents. Kathy wanted to do more outside the building to help students. I was good at meeting with parents to put out fires and deal with sensitive relationships. I was the "go-between" when Kathy met with parents, acting as a facilitator between her and the parent.

The ten years I spent in the Flint school system fulfilled my hope to be a great educator and help urban kids succeed academically and personally. Promoting the success of urban kids became an essential part of who I am as a person and professional educator. *I'm still looking for love and acceptance,* I often thought, *But I'm not sorry I have been concentrating on professional work. I get great satisfaction from teaching, leading, and loving on kids.*

Chapter 6

LIFE IN SPRINGFIELD

I poured myself a glass of wine and wondered if alcohol dependence was in my genes. Or did I drink just because I grew up watching a family of alcoholics and thinking that's just what adults do? I figured it must be some of both. Ever since I was a child, I've been surrounded by adults and drinking. I remember hiding my mother's alcohol and pouring it down the toilet when I was six. I knew first-hand about the destruction that alcohol can inflict upon families. I did not have my first glass of wine until I was a high school senior. When I started drinking in college, at first, it was just socially. Soon after, I was using alcohol to cope with the stress and trauma I continued to endure. I told myself, "Drinking is a way to lighten the load of all the emotional and social baggage I carry with me. I can't get rid of that load easily, but I can bear it when I drink to the point that I don't think about it."

Once I became a teacher, I found out that my experience with trauma could help me relate quickly and deeply with children. But, on the other hand, those experiences made me question whether I would be able to form relationships with colleagues. I had no lasting friends from my childhood since we had moved around so much. However, I formed some friendships in high school, especially with my best friend Sam and her family. Her family loved me and treated me like I was their daughter. It was a safe haven hanging out at their home, where I admired normal family dynamics of always having a seat at their dinner table, watching tv, and getting into trouble with my best friend from time to time!

During my senior year in college, I was having the time of my life; but my drinking had intensified over time. When I went out, the intent was to party and have fun, never to get drunk and not be able to remember what happened— definitely not to have blackouts. I always thought I could outsmart the liquor or beer and be in control. Still, it took many years for me to realize that the only way to beat the consequences of drinking was not to drink at all.

Drinking reflects my personality. For me, it is all or nothing. However, some people are social drinkers and can have just one glass of wine. I could never understand that. It actually made me uncomfortable to be in situations where others were limiting their drinks. Talk about anxiety.

Other people just had one glass of wine or maybe two at parties. I needed a second, third and fourth glass of wine. But I didn't want to draw attention to myself, so I surmised,

"No one's watching what I'm doing because they are talking to each other."

After graduating from Michigan State and accepting my first job as a teacher, I continued to drink from time to time, even while pursuing my master's degree. At first, it was fun; but waking up with a headache from partying was not cool. I knew the stress of life was getting to me. Drinking and driving are not cool and bumping your head in the night is not cool, especially when you wake up with a knot, wondering what happened. Talk about shame and guilt. I thought, *I'm such a horrible, ugly person.* I hated destroying myself. I would resolve not to drink again and then something would happen—a celebration, stress or I just wanted a drink, even if it meant drinking at home alone.

I did go to work hungover, and then, so smart of me, I didn't like the feeling of going to work with my head in the clouds, so I thought, *Why don't I just work my butt off during the week teaching and when I drive back and forth to Michigan State? Then I can be just a weekend drinker!* People who drink put so much thought and planning into their miserable lives and then think they are so smart but fooling themselves! I kept fooling myself. I'd get up, get dressed, do my hair and make-up, put on cute clothes, drive my nice car, work hard, run races, make great friends and co-workers, and while I was at home, I felt utterly broken. This was on the inside; however, outsiders thought I was okay.

Drinking and my mental state made a perfect pair. I don't do moderation. I thought, *I can't just run a marathon; I have to run ten. I can't just get my BA in education; I have to get three graduate degrees, including a doctorate. I can't stay in the classroom; I have to be superintendent. I can't just have one glass of wine; I have to drink the whole bottle. That's who I am.*

I had stayed with my adoptive parents for two years while I finished the teacher certification requirements. When I earned my teaching certificate and got a teaching position in the Flint Community Schools, I moved into an apartment of my own. With a new job and the prospects of being self-supporting, I bought a car—a Grand Am, so I could be an independent student, ready to determine my own future. But actually, I didn't have any money, and my credit was so bad that I couldn't get a car loan. My dad took out a loan so I could buy the car I wanted.

Calvin, the boyfriend I had while in college and who I defended by writing the judge after he went AWOL, returned and moved in with me in my new apartment. I welcomed Calvin, and we became engaged, but we fought and argued. Domestic abuse was part of the relationship. I know now that drinking was one way that I attempted to keep myself together.

During the first couple of years of teaching, I would say, "I'm just tired of drinking."

"No, you're not," Calvin would respond. Then, we would get into a fight. I would say, "I'm trying to figure myself out." Calvin would say, "No, you're not; no, you're not." I would say, "I know because I've grown up around alcoholics all my life. I know all the signs, and I know the behavior I'm exhibiting."

The year before we broke up, Calvin was physically, emotionally, and mentally abusing me. I was doing the same thing to him because hurt people hurt other people. Our relationship was unhealthy, and we broke up because we both realized it was not working. Calvin was eventually admitted to the psychiatric ward at the local hospital. Oftentimes, I still have nightmares about him trying to kill me.

Shortly after Calvin and I separated, my next-door neighbor got robbed and shot. That was enough for me—time to move! So, I moved out and settled in a small community next to Flint. Although I drank heavily on weekends, I sobered up during the week. I continued to find challenge and comfort in my teaching work.

I started thinking about marriage and what it would be like to have a partner to share my life with. I met Terry, who had a wonderful job, at a party hosted by some close friends. After dating for a brief time, we moved in together into a condominium just outside of Flint. At this point, I was assistant principal at Pierce Elementary School. I was used to moving and had no problem resettling. Terry, however, had an ex-girlfriend who kept harassing us. In addition, I had a lot of issues going on at that time with my biological mother and my biological family.

Another problem arose when my Uncle Mike, my mother's brother, and her sister moved to Flint from Florida after Hurricane Noel destroyed their property. My aunt left my uncle, and he moved in with my mother. My aunt eventually returned to Florida, leaving my uncle with my mother, who couldn't care for herself, much less anyone else. Mike also had his own limitations. He was an excessive smoker and had problems walking because of arthritis. It just added to the nightmare I was trying to manage. My mother couldn't take care of Mike, so do you know where he ended up? Living with Terry and me! It didn't last long because my family started accusing me of taking advantage of the situation.

"You're taking Mike's money. You're using Mike's money to pay for your own expenses."

"Wait a minute! I have no interest in that," I shot back. "I don't even want him staying with us." Shortly after, Mike moved to a retirement home where he could be cared for. The situation had been another burden weighing on me, another peg in the playing board of life that convinced me that I had to change my life situation. It left me thinking, *These people are going to drive me crazy, so I've got to get out of here!*

Childhood trauma and stress followed me throughout my adult years. Having finished my master's degree, I worked on an Educational Specialist degree, commuting to classes, and confronting the pressures of all the reading and writing that were part of the program. I was tired and started thinking about giving up alcohol. I began declaring to my friends, "I drink too much, and it's time to stop, refocus, and work on new opportunities."

I love my family dearly, but the stressors of stepping up and stepping in time after time are excruciatingly hurtful. You try so hard, but co-dependent family dynamics were too much for me to handle. With my mother, it was constant. For example, I became her legal guardian. I'm responsible for making sure her bills are paid and that she gets taken care of. I took on this role when I lived in Flint and have continued ever since. At the time, my mother's drinking was so bad that she'd say, "I need $10. I need $20."

"Well, okay, you told me to keep your money for you," I told her. "If I give you this money, then what? There won't be any left!" My mother would call me up to harass me about her money and Uncle Mike's money. It was a mess. It was just one thing after another. It felt like parenting, except this time, the roles were reversed. I was the parent, and my mother was the child. I took care of my mother, trying to keep her out of trouble when I should have been taking care of myself.

Around that time, my younger brother, Sharrod, almost died because his girlfriend came over to my mother's apartment, and they got into a big fight. His girlfriend stabbed him from one end of his chest down to his stomach. When he finally got out of the hospital, who do you think took care of him and stayed with him at his apartment during his recovery? I did! He had staples from just under his rib cage down to his stomach where she had stabbed him. His incision had to be disinfected twice a day. He had to get plenty of rest, so I got him all his meals. His injury reminded me of what happened to my mother. It was precisely the same as when my mother was stabbed by her boyfriend back when I was in high school.

Over the years, I've cultivated a lot of friends. I can create great relationships with people. For instance, Mrs. Roberts was a colleague in Flint when I was a teacher and we ended up becoming longtime friends. I guess being able to lift people up is just one of my strengths. When people come to me and say, "I can't do this!" I would counter their statement with, "Oh yes, you can!" I'm always seen as that person who cares about people. What connects me to them or them to me? I don't know. Many people tell me, "You've done this for me, Kim," or "I admire you, and you've motivated me." My energy and drive bring people to me, and then I use my energy to help them accomplish their goals.

I received my Educational Specialist degree in 2008, capping my second year as assistant principal at Pierce. Around that time, I once again received an unexpected phone call. This call was from the director of human resources in Springfield, another midwestern state. She told me she got my name and information from the Springfield superintendent of schools, who had been the Flint superintendent for about two years. The superintendent told the director of human resources to call me and talk about some opportunities they had in Springfield. She offered me a guidance dean position, and I accepted.

After twelve years of professional growth, continued education and climbing the professional ladder, I resigned from Flint Community Schools. I enjoyed the two years of learning administrative work at Pierce School. However, the principal did not want me to leave. So, when I left, I told her that the new job was an opportunity to expand my horizons that I couldn't turn down.

At the same time, I realized it was a way to escape the problems I felt trapped in and overwhelmed by while living in Flint. My mother's drinking and health problems continued, along with her hospitalization. I was drinking too much myself in the evenings and on weekends. I recognized I was drinking again to alleviate the pressure from work and despondence over the never-ending family problems. Love for my mother translated into caring for her when she was well enough to function at home and grieving for her when she had to be hospitalized yet again. I felt obligated to help my siblings as they continued to face challenges in their own lives.

Although I felt some guilt about leaving my mom and my siblings, I wanted to be in a place where I could focus on my own life. While I was establishing myself as a professional educator, I realized that family matters had drained my energy. I was in and out of relationships, which caused me to question myself. "Am I ever going to find someone I can build a lasting relationship with?" I envied my sister, who had children she loved and loved her. "Would that ever happen to me?" I wondered. The prospects in Flint seemed slim.

I've always been one to expand my horizons. As I grew older, I became more open to finding what was out there in the world and not just staying in Flint. I was optimistic in Flint, but eventually, the family part wore me down, even more than my job. I was ready for a change.

Chapter 7
STUDENTS FIRST

The phone rang, and the Director of Human Resources was on the other end. "This is Cynthia. I'm calling to ask you to come to Springfield to work with us. You know the superintendent here, Dr. Milton. He suggested I call you. I need you as the principal at Harvard Park Elementary School. We need someone good here to help us move this school system in a more successful direction. We know you and your work in Flint, and we think you are the person for this."

"Yes! I'll take it," I answered immediately. She explained that the school needed someone to get it under control and work constructively with the teachers and community. This opportunity was not only a way out of Flint but a promotion from assistant principal to principal. It would be one more step up the administrative ladder. I was ready.

I hung up and thought, *A great opportunity! But it is so far from home. What is Springfield like? I need to know something about where I'm going.* So, I started to look up information about the place.

I learned that Springfield, located "downstate," as they say there, was a bit larger than Flint. Its white population was about twice the size of Flint's, and the Black population was less than half the size. Springfield was on the fabled Route 66 highway, which attracted many visitors. Flint had only a few, and they mainly attracted local people. Springfield offered more diverse work opportunities, and their pay was better.

I was so excited. I felt that going to Springfield would be a new adventure because it held the potential for career advancement. Springfield offered opportunities to explore an environment that was more promising than Flint, a city on the decline. Yet, I would be leaving family, friends and familiarity with my surroundings. Still, I was ready to move away due to the family issues I confronted so regularly. Even though it was a big gamble, I was excited about accepting the job offer.

I called a former colleague who had worked with me in Flint. He took a job as principal in Springfield the previous year.

"You're going to love it here," he told me. "Don't worry about getting settled. I'll help you meet people."

The first week after my contract ended with Flint schools, I packed my things, put some in the basement at my sister's house, got in my car, and drove to Springfield. It took a while to get there. Finally, I checked in at a motel, ready to find an apartment and go to work. I called my friend, hoping he could assist with some housing options. But he was already gone for the summer.

The next morning, I went directly to the superintendent's office to let him know I was there and ready to work. The first thing he said was, "This is going to be a tough job. I hope you understand what you have agreed to do." I laughed and said, "I'm from Flint, a city of tough people! So, let's get started!"

He introduced me to people in the office, and they all said they were glad that I was there. But, like many challenges in my life, this all didn't work out like I thought it would. After a couple of weeks of finding a place to live and settling in, I got another call from the superintendent. He asked me to see him again. When I got to his office, I sat down.

"I am sorry, but the principal at Harvard Park Elementary School isn't leaving," he said. My heart almost stopped. I thought I was going to throw up. I had quit my job in Flint and didn't have any place to go. But before I could say anything, he told me he had another job for me that was especially important to the system. He told me that the opening was at a middle school and had the title of "guidance dean."

Walter explained, "The guidance dean provides academic advising to middle school students and assists in classroom observations when the principal requests this. You will take charge of the graduation ceremony, student of the week, and honors recognition. You'll be responsible for supervising and enforcing attendance procedures, supervising the behavior and safety of students getting on and off of buses, and will oversee the cafeteria and extra-curricular activities. You will handle requests by parents for community resources and facilitate parent conferences, including individual plans for students who need extra academic or social support."

I absorbed this message with surprise, wonder, doubt and some relief. Yes, I had known Dr. Milton when he was the superintendent in Flint. We had worked together for two years, in which I held a variety of positions. Yes, he knew I was good at teaching, being a leader, and taking command of problems that needed fixing. He knew I was well-liked, even though I was direct and demanded others live up to their responsibilities. But, since I dreamed of being an administrator and potentially a district superintendent, this position—like the principalship, was an opportunity to move in that direction. It would make it possible for me to become known at the district and community levels.

I stepped into my position as guidance dean with my usual determination to resolve problems and work towards positive change. For example, I noticed right away that open conversations about the need for tracking and targeting

Black male students were a standard, negative practice. When I went into the teachers' lounge and attended their meetings, I heard them say things like, "A lot of these kids just don't have what it takes to get good grades. They mess around in class and never do their homework. Some of them come and sleep in class. What's the matter with their parents? Don't they care about helping their kids? I don't see how we can help them if they don't care, and their parents don't care either. We should put the kids who want to learn in one or two sections so the teachers can concentrate on them."

During the second week of school, I witnessed one incident of a Black male student being put up against the wall, legs spread apart, and arms sprawled against the wall as if he were to be arrested. I couldn't believe what I was seeing. Heart pounding with anger, I walked over and demanded, "Tell me what's going on here!" The guards quickly released the student from that position.

The student was sent back to class, and I asked the security guards to tell me what had happened that caused them to treat a student in that way. They told me, "When we see something that looks like a problem, we always have students up against the wall like that." I had also seen it plenty of times when I lived in Flint, especially in situations with some of my high school African American male classmates. I knew it was scary and degrading for them. In this instance in Springfield, the security guards were convinced that this was correct school practice and that I had interfered. So, the message to me was Black male students with hoodies on equaled trouble, and I wasn't buying it!

I went directly to the principal, who showed me the school rules. The rules clarified that the procedure I saw was not permissible unless the student was a clear and dangerous threat to other students or teachers. Next, the principal and I met with the security guards. We worked out a different procedure that gave students a chance to explain what they had been doing that had alarmed the security guards. We also formulated several follow-up procedures to use depending on the situation. I sensed a slightly more positive attitude among the students after the changes in the disciplinary procedures went into effect.

One of my favorite parts of the job was meeting with parents. They had so many ideas about what would help their children do better in school.

"My daughter doesn't understand why she should learn what you're teaching. Give her reading about Black kids, and she will pay more attention. Tell my son how the math will help him in his own life."

"Ask the kids what they think they need to learn."

I listened and started infusing my ideas about how to incorporate the parents and my own thinking about making learning culturally relevant into the curriculum.

The school counselor was professionally one of the best I ever worked with because she came to meetings with the parents whenever I needed her help. In addition, she was great at working with the students and their teachers. In general, this job gave me an excellent chance to get to know community members and helped me fit well into the school system.

At the beginning of my second year, four days before the students came back, I was in a teachers' meeting when the school secretary came in and told me to call the superintendent right away. His message was short.

"I need you to be the principal at Harvard Park Elementary School. Get that school under control."

This was the same school where I thought I would be principal when I came the year before. Like some of the other Springfield elementary schools, it had low test scores and needed someone who would bring discipline, directness and high expectations for both the students and the staff. But unlike other schools in the state that had about fifteen percent African American students, Harvard Park had about fifty percent. More than ninety percent of the students were eligible for free lunch. Twenty-eight percent were considered learning disabled, a much higher percentage than in most schools in that state. With a staff of about thirty, the school serviced about 500 pre-K to fifth-grade students. The school was built in the early 1900s. It was closed for several years in the depression and later reopened as the area gained businesses and population. As soon as I became principal, I started to work with teachers, students, and parents to improve test scores to meet or exceed state standards.

I had little time to prepare for my role as principal. However, as a person with high energy and high expectations, I did not waste any time before assuming leadership responsibilities. New challenges confronted me immediately. To start the new school year, I was responsible for all the teachers' and staff meetings. I needed to start by focusing on the meetings necessary to begin the school year positively. There wasn't much time since school would open in only four days. As I prepared for the meetings, I thought, "I will never do this again by myself. The teachers, staff and community will be involved in planning for these meetings from now on."

The first week after the students returned, my assistant principal came running and told me that a student had started a fire in the boys' bathroom. My heart was pounding as I ran to the scene. In all my years of working in urban schools, nothing like that had ever happened. As I ran into the bathroom, I saw flames and smoke. The student had set the trash can on fire. I put the fire out with the extinguisher I grabbed from the hall. In the back of my mind, I wondered, *Why in the hell didn't the assistant principal put it out?* Immediately, I called the student's mother, who was at work.

"Come to school right away! I need to talk to you about a fire your son set in school today." I also called the fire department, and they sent someone over to talk to him about fire safety. After the mother arrived, I suspended the student for ten days.

"You have to get him to a counselor within the ten days that he will be out of school," I told her. "I have to have proof that he is being seen by a counselor before I will let him return." Some people thought I should have expelled him. I thought about it, but I didn't want to do what had been done in the past to no avail. I needed to give this student a second chance. I told the mother I had put my job on the line for him. Even though there was a rule, and I am not a rule follower, I thought *I would work with my students and their families to make this school a safe place that they want to come to and take care of. I can do this some other way, not by just expelling the student. I was going to lead with love the way I always had.*

That was my first week on the job, and I thought, *What the hell? This kid just tried to burn down the school!* But the student in question came back and turned into a model student. His mother had other kids, and every time she saw me, she said, "Thanks." Students just needed someone to put their neck out for them. I had work to do.

I worked on building effective communication and relationships with parents to get them to support the school and me and help their children learn. These relationships developed over time and eventually paid off in better learning results. For instance, the parent educator, whose job was to work with groups of parents to help them find ways to support their kids, told me about one student that she thought was being sexually abused. I had noticed this student, too, and was worried about him. He was incredibly quiet and stayed away from the other kids, especially during recess. He was also quick to anger if someone bothered him.

I called the student's mother in for conferences several times and expressed my concerns about him. The mother would just say, "Oh, there is nothing wrong with him. He is just behaving that way." The third time the mother came up to the school, she finally admitted that her son had been abused. I told the mother I had no choice but to call Child Protective Services.

"You don't have to guess. I am telling you I will call them," I said to the mother. "If you want to be angry with someone, you can be angry with me. Now we all know this is happening, and you have known in the past that this boy was being abused." I told her that no matter what CPS did, she had to get him into counseling right away. This was not something that was going to go away in a few sessions; it could take counseling for the rest of his life.

"You have to take him right away," I admonished her.

"Oh, Ms. Leverette. Okay, okay, okay. I will take him right away." And she did.

Another time, one of my fifth-grade students brought a knife to school. I secured the knife and immediately called his mother to my office with the social worker, teacher, and assistant principal. The student explained that no one was bothering him, but he didn't feel safe walking to school. So, he kept the knife in his backpack for protection to and from school. His mother cried and pleaded with me not to expel her son. This kid was on the honor roll, well-behaved, had good attendance, and had no referrals. I suspended him for ten days, and mom went with her son to counseling. I arranged for the activity bus to take him at the end of the day and mom said she would be able to drive him to school. He was a great kid who I gave another chance! He is now a college graduate and doing well!

I connected with students' parents regularly. For instance, when a local church was giving away gift cards at Christmas, I noticed them giving a gift card to one of the parents I knew who spent money on cigarettes, even when she didn't have enough money. Within hearing distance of the people from the church, I told the parent, "I'm going to the store with you so I can make sure you don't spend any of it on cigarettes." Then, one of the church people spoke up.

"You're going to take her to the grocery store?"

"Yes," I said. "I will make sure she doesn't get any cigarettes with that money."

"Wow! We don't know any administrators who do that sort of thing."

"Well, that is what we do here," I said as I smiled and went off to the store. "We are family here."

During my first year at HP, I noticed that students were not eager to come to school. The kids didn't behave, the teachers had low morale, and the test scores were below state standards. I realized that my staff and I needed to do something to make school "fun." Knowing that there were no sports in the elementary schools in the district, I decided that I needed to change that. I told the staff, "You know me. I come from a city that is the heart of *basketball*! So, we will make two basketball teams, and we will just play each other."

We started basketball at Harvard Park with lots of enthusiasm. In addition to the two teams, we had cheerleaders. One of the girls who wanted to be a cheerleader was much heavier than the other students. The cheerleader selection committee consisted of a teacher, my secretary, and the parent educator. They told her right away that she would not be a cheerleader. I told the committee that this was not right.

"She will be a cheerleader as long as I have anything to say about it!" I told them. "She is going to be on the squad. This is not about cute girls doing the splits or jumping around and waving pompoms. She is going to be on the team!" I know that I stepped in and took their power away. At the time, I didn't care why they didn't want her—she was larger and wouldn't be able to do the things the others could, which they assumed, but I knew it would boost her self-esteem being on the squad. She might never get to be on a cheerleading squad again, but at least she would be able to say, "When I was in the fifth grade, I was on the cheerleading team." The committee members walked away muttering.

She stayed on the team that first year. She didn't make the team the second year, but it didn't matter much because the seed was already planted. What being a cheerleader did for her self-esteem that first year was great. For example, that's what these inclusion things are all about. I thought it was amazing to see her come out of that experience and see her confidence soar. At the end of the day, it was priceless. I thought it had been worth my saying, "If this kid isn't on the cheerleading team, then we won't have cheerleaders." I had been her principal while she was with me in second through sixth grade, and I just loved her so much.

One of the local churches was looking for a way to reach out to the schools as a service to the community. They wanted to help significantly way beyond simply providing food and treats for school events. The other schools turned down their offer to help, but I seized upon it when they contacted me. I got them to donate everything the cheerleaders and basketball team needed, from socks to shirts to shorts.

After the first year, the other schools also formed teams, and they wanted to play Harvard Park. I jokingly told my students that they would end up in detention if they didn't have an undefeated year. We did have an undefeated year. The teachers and parents wanted to know if I actually told the team that. I said, "Yes, but it was a joke!" Our team played eight other schools in the district and won all the games. Everyone was out to get us the second year, and we went undefeated again. If I were a principal today, I know I could not get away with making such a joke; but at the time, I knew it would give the kids motivation and spirit as a team. They knew I was serious about wanting them to play hard and play to win, but they also knew they would not get punished if they didn't.

When we went undefeated the first year, I arranged a banquet for the students. Like so many educators, I bought a huge cake and trophy out of my own money. When the Parent Educator told me that the Title I director had called and asked if we had spent Title I funds for the snacks and napkins, she asked, "How should I respond?" I told her not to respond at all.

"We don't use Title I or II funds for trophies," I explained. "If he wants to come over here to the party, he can. I don't have time for that kind of nonsense. We are celebrating kids and their successes."

I understood that educational systems—particularly in low-income schools, were not working to support students' learning. It was not just at Harvard Park and other schools in Springfield; it was also the case in Flint. This realization led me to adamantly proclaim, "There is something wrong with the system! There is something wrong with the system!" So here I was, working night and day to make things better at Harvard Park. I worked to improve the students' social and academic experiences by following the rules and figuring out how to get volunteers and contributions. Someone called me to ensure I didn't spend Title I funds on napkins. It was ridiculous to treat me that way. I knew that if you were liked by people "higher up," you got favors, but if you were doing things differently—despite getting good results, you were suspected of doing something wrong. You were threatening the complacency of other people in the school system, and they resented that. It meant they might have to start working harder themselves.

I also realized that even though I couldn't fix everything wrong, I was making a difference for the students at the other district schools. I was tired out, but I worked on weekends to achieve my goals of school improvement. Others would see my car at the school and tell me, "Go home!" but I stayed.

At the end of my first year of being a principal, I called one of my professors—one of the professors who gave me rent money when I was so broke that first semester of my internship. I wanted to get her help in thinking about how to help my teachers develop their classroom and our school culture so that it was more cohesive, supportive, and working towards common goals. She sent me two books about classroom learning communities and the other about professional learning communities. After reading them, I changed the teacher meetings the following school year from focusing on traditional messages from the principal to developing knowledge and skills that the teachers wanted to pursue. It took time, but we learned to work together as a professional learning community. For instance, we worked out a helpful way of using student records. It helped us all to use student data so that plans for classroom learning could be focused on individual student learning and applying knowledge and skills across subject matter. In addition, we learned what we could do with the students that supported their self-control development and working constructively with other classmates. After a few months, I felt a change of attitudes throughout the school. I saw students and teachers helping their peers learn. I felt like I had accomplished a tremendous change for the good.

Everything was not easy, however. One teacher was unsuccessful with her students academically or creating an effective classroom learning community culture. She sent many students who were acting out to see the counselor or to my office rather than dealing with the situation herself. Her students' academic scores had not improved over several years. To add to the problems, she was often absent. She used all her sick leave every year.

I wanted to fire her, but I realized I didn't have a process for doing this. Then, I remembered that some students in my college cohort dropped out of their internships. Once again, I called two of my professors and talked with them about how the professors "fired" the interns who weren't making it. The professors said they didn't kick out students who were having a terrible time. Instead, they talked with the intern about why the intern wanted to be a teacher. They all had distinct reasons for being in the program, but none genuinely wanted to be a teacher. One was there because his parents wanted him to be a teacher, but he had never been interested in teaching. Another said it was the only program where she could get a scholarship. The conversations helped the interns figure out what they really wanted to do and what other programs they could explore. Ultimately, these students were happy because their explorations and decisions helped them change their majors.

I decided to have a similar conversation with my teacher, who had problems. I learned that she was a teacher because she hadn't had a chance to change careers while she was in college. She had not been interested in her education degree at all. After talking with me a few times, she told me that her husband was highly interested in helping her find a new job. She said she would leave during the school year but would stay until the end of the year if that was what was needed. I decided to hire a long-term substitute who I knew would connect well with the class and get them to learn. I heard that the teacher who left found an editing job she enjoyed. The students started paying better attention in class, and their grades improved when they had a consistent and caring teacher.

I was still running. Running sustained me physically, emotionally and mentally. Running was therapeutic because it reduced my stress. I also realized that I needed that school as much as it needed me. I could sublimate the thoughts and emotions I had brought from my life in Flint because I was so focused on my work. Having brought about change and influenced principals in the other elementary schools, I could say to myself, "Now, at last, I can look at the children and think, 'you've got a chance.'" As broken as I was, there was no better person, in my view, to send to HP than me. I had loads of energy, emotion and devotion that I was using to invest in all the children.

When I started working in the district, all I did was work. There were so many professional items on my bucket list that I had to set my personal wishes aside. Instead, I focused on becoming a great educator and helping urban kids succeed academically. I was also making progress as a principal and a potential superintendent. I had reached my goal to be a principal, and I had made an enormous difference in that school. As my professional life became more successful and less stressful, I began to work more on my personal life. My wish to get married and have a family became increasingly central to my thinking.

Chapter 8

DREAMS FULFILLED

W hen I received the call from the personnel director in Springfield concerning the position, I jumped at it. I recognized it was my chance to get away. But the result was more significant changes in my personal life than I had ever imagined. Not only did I find new friends that grew out of my work with school and church, but I also met a man and fell in love.

Having accepted the new job, I expected to socialize with the superintendent, his wife, their friends, and a former Flint colleague who moved to Springfield. I knew I would be alone, but I didn't anticipate being lonely because these people were there. I had never been really far from home before. When I went to college, I was only forty-five miles from home and my dad, whom I relied upon for emotional and financial support.

Right away, in Springfield, I realized my social life wouldn't be what I expected. Initially, I was lonely. Moreover, my assumptions about my social relationships with my former Flint colleagues did not work out as I thought. As a result, I did not socialize with them. Instead, I gradually became acquainted with new colleagues and new neighbors and developed friendships among them. Nevertheless, these relationships took time to grow.

Professionally, I excelled in my work in Springfield. Although not on solid ground yet, I had stopped drinking and was open to meeting new people in an unfamiliar environment. I suddenly became a school principal just before school started the second year. I was thrown into situations that had me interacting with numerous people such as the Harvard Park teachers, parents, and other district principals. I found a significant difference between the jobs of guidance dean and elementary school principal. As principal, my associations with many school personnel, parents, and other Springfield people expanded quickly.

One of the most fortuitous events provided much-needed support for the school and for me personally. It came from a local Christian church. As I described in the previous chapter, the parishioners were searching for a school to work with as an outreach project. While none of the other schools they approached accepted their offer, I did not hesitate to say, "Yes!"

I developed a partnership with Westside Church, a predominantly white church, while our school was fifty percent non-white. As a result, the church understood what it meant to truly be a partner.

The first person I met from the church was Melissa. During Christmas time, Melissa organized one of the church's first activities at Harvard Park. The church people put together two weeks' worth of food for every family at the school. Melissa said, "We'll put everything in the gym, so there is plenty of room for the families to come and get what they need."

"Okay," I responded. Then, I just watched, hoping that the families would come, and they did.

It took no time for Melissa and me to connect. Finally, I had a chance to see what the church was doing in terms of their behavior, interaction with the staff, and interactions with the students and their families. It was genuine, and it touched me deeply because as a kid, I got help from the Old News Boys at the Flint Journal. When kids of poverty are supported in this way, they receive a gift from the Old News Boys at Christmastime. When I was growing up, I always received a sweater, gloves, and underwear—those kinds of basic needs—from the Old News Boys. I will never forget that. Now, I am able to volunteer and support great causes like those.

I remember walking through and shopping at Goodwill. I know what it's like to receive those things when you're not fortunate enough to have anything. When people do something for me, I remind myself, "They don't have to do this." The people from the church did it out of their love for God, for HP students, and their families. That meant a lot to me.

One of my missions was to help students increase their sense of self-esteem and purpose. When I decided to start a basketball team at the school, knowing that the parents could not afford expensive uniforms and equipment, I searched for other ways to acquire these necessities. The church was eager to help. As the church got involved, I became friends with several of them. When they invited me to attend church, I accepted. I became a regular member and found lasting friendships there.

My friendship with Melissa really took root during those first years at HP. Melissa was about my age, married, and starting a family. She invited me to join a church group going on a mission trip to Kenya. Having already experienced the thrill of traveling internationally when I studied abroad in France, I was enthusiastic about going abroad again, this time to an African country. I had never imagined that such an opportunity would cross my path. I knew one of the HP teachers who went the first year that the church sponsored this mission trip. She and others from the church returned, sharing their excitement and stories about their experiences. "Bring the Light" was what they said. I wondered, *Bring the light? What is 'Bring the light'?*

When that HP teacher came back from Kenya, talking about instructing poor children at a school there, I realized *I needed to do this. I want to do it to be part of something much bigger than what is going on at Harvard Park.* So, I attended an informational meeting, and afterward, I said, "I'm going!" The church organizers were surprised and flattered that the principal wanted to go. I quickly became an enthusiastic participant as a group member and its mission. Not one to set stone in titles like "principal," I discouraged the other participants from deferring to my ideas and judgment just because I held a position of authority in their eyes.

I went twice, two years in a row. Part of my motivation to go was my desire to show Westside Church I deeply cared about their involvement with Harvard Park students and families. I had been so impressed with what the church had done to help the Harvard Park students. Now, I had the opportunity to have the adventure of a lifetime and do service for the church where I felt so accepted.

Members of Westside who had been missionaries and had traveled in Africa were responsible for organizing the trip. Participants had to pay for their own expenses. The trip was fourteen days. We took books, especially children's literature, a supply of vaccines, and lots of clothes for the people we were there to help. I was inspired to empty out as much of my closet as possible!

The missionary group arrived in Nairobi, Kenya. We stayed in a hotel, but the work took place in the Masai areas of the Rift Valley in a couple of different villages. We worked in elementary and middle schools for children. Each morning, I got up early so I could run before the group got up for breakfast. The hotel owners in Nairobi told us where to run and shop. I kept pinching myself as I ran, saying, "I'm in Africa, and I'm running!" After breakfast, we got on a bus that drove us to the villages, picked us up after dinner at night, and returned to the hotel. During the evening, we met as a group and talked about the day and our tasks for the next day.

Each of us had different jobs and responsibilities. For example, I was a member of the education component and was responsible for preparing lesson plans with expected outcomes. I was also responsible for going over the teaching plans each day with the teachers who taught elementary grade level children and helping teachers with problems. In addition, we had dentists, nurses, and doctors on this trip.

My impressions of the children in the village where we worked were vivid. It was inspiring to see children who lacked so much yet showed their happiness and love for God even though they lived in extreme poverty. The kids were jumping all over the classroom when they came in. They were trying to get to the front of the room! I thought, *Wow! I had no idea children would be so eager to be at school. How can I make this happen at all schools?*

The kids didn't have toilets to use, so they used the side of the road and lived with other deprivations such as no running water in their houses. I got on the bus with my "shades" on because I didn't want people to see I was crying. I cried every day, and I cried every night. I also came to see how huge God is and how they still loved God even in extreme poverty. They kept talking about "Bring the light."

Finally, I found out what "Bring the light" meant. Part of the work was to go to the village and pray with a family in their home. We talked about God's love and that He brought light to any darkness. Their houses had corrugated metal roofs and little light entered the living space except through the door. After talking with a family, the men from Westside and some from the village got on top of the roof, cut a square, and covered the square with fiberglass. Then light shown into the house. That's what they called "Bring the light." When I first had that experience, I understood that just by cutting a hole in the roof, we were acting as the hands and feet of God by changing the physical light. It also brought light into our hearts as we worked together to accomplish these improvements.

We worked from sunup to sundown. After dinner, members of the Masai tribe came out to the village where we were working. They really took to me. I realized that they were comfortable with me because of the similarity in our skin color. I also took to them because they would joke with me while we walked around.

"You should be in the front of the line. How could you let all these white people get in front?" I was just trying to keep up. In fact, I often had to literally catch my breath because the elevation was so high there.

The children I worked with spoke fairly good English. During all the years of working in U.S. schools, I had never seen students so eager to learn. As always, I grew attached to the students I worked with. I decided to sponsor a little girl named Anna, and I actually met her. Although she was about five years old, she appeared to be two years old because she was so malnourished. Unfortunately, her family ended up leaving the valley, which meant I could no longer sponsor her. Still, I decided to sponsor another child through an organization that handles such sponsorships. For me, it was a very fulfilling experience.

At the end of the mission trip, we got to go on a beautiful safari. We saw animals like I'd never seen—right out of *The National Geographic*. You go from a place of material deprivation to a beautiful safari. *I'm so privileged to be in such an exotic place and have these life-changing experiences,* I thought. *God is great!*

I chose to return on the second trip so I could see the child I sponsored and do the church's mission work. The second trip was about the same as the first. The Kenyan village people were so excited when they found out that I had come back for the second year. Again, that year, church participants did dentistry and bible education. I did a leadership challenge and coached some teachers. The challenge involved engaging in activities that required taking risks to develop decision-making skills. We also worked on team development and problem-solving by doing simulated activities and critiquing the results. For example, we formed two groups of lower elementary teachers and two of upper elementary. Each group had to design a project geared toward their students' grade level to beautify the school grounds. When the groups presented their projects, each said they got along well together and wanted to implement their plan as soon as possible.

"Who wants to stop in Paris? I do!" After the second trip, another teacher and I stopped in Paris on the way back for an overnight stay. This trip was different from the trip I took as a graduate student. I had enough income this time, so the money aspect of stopping in Paris was not the same. When we landed at the Charles de Gaulle airport, which is a long way from the center of Paris, we took public transportation to the hotel. A passenger on the plane had told us that the taxi ride from the airport to the center city was outrageously expensive, so we decided to be adventurous and take the Metro. That was a learning experience in itself, but luckily it was rather easy to figure out. We spent the afternoon, evening, and next morning simply walking around the streets. We stopped in small shops and window shopped. The restaurants we ate in were small and looked family-owned, but the food was great.

Back in Springfield, I still desired to become a superintendent. So, I went beyond my master's and Educational Specialist degrees to pursue a doctorate at Maryville University in St. Louis, Missouri. I graduated in 2013 with my mother in attendance at the degree conferring ceremony. As I looked at the audience during the ceremony, I thought, *I can't believe my mom came all the way from Flint to be here. I feel like this is a way for my mom to say she is proud of me and loves me.* This time, I could see her beautiful smile and her eyes smiling and saying, "I love you, Kim."

Moving to Springfield was one of the smartest things I did to make professional and personal changes. New life was breathed into my personal life. I enjoyed the friendships I was developing with my church colleagues. The two trips to Kenya meant a lot to me since I got to see another part of the world, and I got to meet some wonderful people there. When my mother came to my doctoral graduation, I felt so happy that she had made the trip and stayed sober. All I needed was to fall in love and start a family of my own.

Chapter 9

DREAM TO NIGHTMARE

In addition to finding new friends, my love life also blossomed. In the back of my mind and heart, I wanted to get married and have a family. One day in the spring of my first year there, I walked into a garden nursery, looking for some foliage to plant around my apartment. I saw a handsome man named Kevin and talked with him about the plants. By chance, he was a professional landscaper, originally from Jamaica but living in the U.S. for over twenty years and was now a citizen.

Kevin and I started dating. As I got to know him, I was attracted to his work ethic and other qualities I admired. He had his own profitable business, saved his money, owned his home, and traveled worldwide. He challenged me to save money, which I wanted to do so that I could buy a house for my mother. Eventually, because Kevin had helped me in this way, I was able to pay cash for a house for her in Flint.

Kevin was a great cook. I liked that he was a vegetarian and became one myself. Although he was a heavy drinker, he was a really nice person when he wasn't drinking. So, when he asked me to marry him, I said, "Yes!"

About six months after we met, we were married on the beach in Trinidad, Tobago. We chose Trinidad because Kevin loved to travel, and he had been to the Bahamas and Jamaica several times. Trinidad was a place we always wanted to visit. I wore a beautiful wedding dress. It was just the two of us and the Justice of the Peace. There were no attendants because no one in my family could get there or any of my new friends could come. We stayed for two weeks in a little house by the beach. After the honeymoon, we went to Flint because my family and friends wanted to give us a shower.

Coming from a single-parent, dysfunctional family, I had not experienced a constructive marriage or seen how couples worked through problems. Therefore, I soon had a challenging time living with my husband. I thought that it was partly because I was not used to having someone telling me what to do or having to do what other people wanted. I had lived by myself all my adult life and made decisions based on what I wanted to do and what I believed would be productive for me. Given that I had moved to escape being around people who drank and had begun to believe this habit was unacceptable, I could hardly believe that I had managed to get myself into yet another troubled relationship.

As the relationship deteriorated, I finally realized that I was not making any progress in improving it. So, one Christmas, I went back to Flint to see my family. While I was there, I had lunch with three of my friends. When I told them how I was being treated, they became overly concerned.

"Kim, what's going on? What's he doing to you? Does he hit you? Are you safe with him? What do you do to get back at him?" This discussion helped me see more clearly what was wrong.

I became even more aware of the problems in my marriage when I received a teaching award from the College of Education at Michigan State. This award was given to about twenty people each year who had been nominated by someone who wanted the recipient recognized as an outstanding educator. I was surprised to be nominated, thinking, *That's something for other people.* I was impressed by the recognition and honor it brought me. As I was about to leave to attend the award dinner, Kevin announced, "I'm not going with you." I was deeply shaken by his refusal to attend. As I was driving down the highway, I thought, *I could get into an accident right now because I was so devastated, and I was not focused on my driving.* I was crying so much that the tears blurred my vision. *I can't understand how he can let me go all the way home to accept this award without going with me!* That's when I realized he would do anything he could to break my spirit. But just because I knew what he was doing didn't mean I would actually take any action to protect myself. Still, the handwriting was on the wall, so to speak. When I got back to Springfield, I hardly spoke to Kevin and just went about my work.

Some people told me that I didn't give my marriage enough time, but I said, "No. It was wrong from the time I got into it." I was so anxious to get married and start a family. I wanted to be in what I thought was a "normal family." For the first several months, I was still in the "honeymoon" mode, but when the fight and lack of real affection became more evident to me, I became more defiant and self-reliant.

Looking back, I had stopped drinking, and he was a drinker. I have to admit that I saw that dichotomy even before we married. Afterward, I thought, *Why did I get married when there were signs of discord already there?* For example, one of the times we went out to dinner, I saw how he treated the waitress, giving her a tough time. He said things like, "Why does it take you so long to bring our food? You should refill my wine glass more quickly." That bothered me tremendously. It was not that there were problems with our food or anything. He just tried to intimidate people. Those kinds of things bother me. I felt like he was trying to break me down and control me.

I was devastated and hurt that this person I loved would not support me. There was no physical abuse; it was all verbal and mental abuse. Right after we got married, he wanted me to come home around 4:00—as soon as the schools were out; however, I needed to be at other places for my work. It got so bad to where he would call the administration building, and they told him I got out at 4:00 pm. By the time 5:00 p.m. or 6:00 p.m. rolled around, and I still wasn't home, he became furious. I kept telling him that it was my job to be out in schools after leaving the administration office. I couldn't just work and then run home at 4:00 p.m. Because Kevin owned his own business, he could set his own hours and control his work time better than I could. He wanted me home when he was home, mostly so he could have a drink in my company. It got to the point that when I got home and put the key in the door, I knew there would be an argument of some kind. I cried all the time.

Shortly after we were married, I had a scare with a mammogram. I came home, trying to explain how upset and worried I was. Instead, he laughed at me. I probably didn't sleep for two weeks. It was that kind of thing that hurt me to my core and made me really angry. I told him things about my family and how I grew up. He would say, "That's because your whole family is crazy, and your mother is especially crazy." I realize now that he was just being spiteful. Those kinds of things made me more resentful and wanting to pull away. When I found out that I didn't have breast cancer, all he said was, "So, no big deal." I was devastated and didn't speak to him for the rest of the night.

I had thought it was too early in the marriage for counseling. He might have a different story, but I felt like it was all manipulation, and everything was my fault. That's how he made me feel—everything was my fault. I finally got him to agree to see a marriage counselor, but we only went twice. The therapist was looking at me like, "What have you got yourself into?"

"I'm sorry, this is not going to work," I told the therapist. "We're not coming back. This is not going to work." Counseling only added to the frustration. I kept going to church, and he wouldn't go to church with me. That was another thing we argued about. We had different views about religion, and we were not equally yoked.

When I moved into his house, we never ever made it "our house." I put all my stuff in storage. I had to just make things work.

"This is your house and I feel like a roommate," I said to him. "I don't feel like we are two people who got married and really love each other." The more we tried and the harder I tried, the worse it got.

The last straw was when we went to Chicago for a weekend. He got drunk and he didn't come back to our hotel room. This was not the first time he'd done something like this. I wondered, *What is taking him so long to come back?* I went down to the lobby, and I found him arguing with the security guard. I thought, *Here we go again.* The manager told me I could stay, but my husband had to leave. He drove to Flint, where he dropped me off, and he left.

"I don't know why you're so concerned about what people think," he said. "That's stupid." I'm thinking to myself, *Are you crazy? I have a career. I have a reputation. Yes, I do care about how people think. You are out in public picking a fight with people because, basically you are intoxicated. In this day and age, people can so easily video record a scene or take a picture. I don't need anyone exposing my personal life on Facebook or some other medium.* In my position as a public-school administrator, I had to be mindful of my reputation, both professionally and personally. I finally admitted that I never knew what kind of person he would be once he started drinking. I just knew one thing; it wasn't going to be good.

That marriage was one of the most debilitating experiences I've ever had. It failed, and it should have.

Before we got married, I was totally in denial about the shape our relationship was taking. As the marriage fell apart, I woke up one Saturday morning crying and thinking, *I can't go back. I can't stay with him any longer.*

I should have known better since I had grown up seeing my mom and her boyfriend fighting all the time. My siblings also experienced physical abuse in their relationships with their partners. I wasn't looking for an abusive relationship but ended up in one anyway. At least I wasn't hurt physically, but emotionally and mentally, I was shattered. I started calling home, talking to my sister, brothers, and mother. My mother said to me, "You are my daughter. I love the ground you walk on." To me, that equaled, "I love you." In fact, it is even stronger than saying, "I love you." Then she gave me advice and said, "You will not make the same mistakes with your life that I made with mine. So, I want you to pack up immediately. If you need me to get a ride and come down there to make that happen, I will. You just tell me what you need me to do. You have worked too hard. You have a distinguished career, you know how to take care of yourself, and you need to leave if this is going on."

That conversation gave me the strength that I needed. My brothers and my sister said the same thing. It was almost like an intervention. It was the first time my mother clearly voiced her concern. She was proud of me. She was the strength that I needed at the time. I got off the phone with her and did exactly what she told me to do. I left.

If it weren't for my mother telling me to leave, I don't know where I would be today. How ironic it was that it was my mother who said, "You've got to get out of there." I had always been the one who gave people advice, but now they were calling me saying, "Did you decide to leave?" Today, I still remember how traumatic it all was.

I had needed to hear that concern from my family for a long time. Finally, I saw that they cared. They saw and recognized that I needed their support. There were so many other times that I just wanted to scream, "I have to be strong." However, I needed to be taken care of this time, and my family recognized that. I had never had enough time to think about myself because I always cared for other people. This time, I needed someone to take care of me for a change.

I don't know why, but Melissa from Westside Church texted me.

Hi friend! How are you doing?

Can you call me? I texted back, and she did right away. With tears rolling down my cheeks, I said, "What am I going to do? What am I going to do? I'm in bad shape. I'm just going along.

I don't know what to do. I can't stay at my husband's house. I have to find a place to live." She said, "Meet me at the church." I sort of hesitated. She said, "Kim, can you meet me at the church? I just want to talk to you."

At the church, I told her what was going on with my husband. I basically spilled out my guts to her about the fights Kevin and I were having and that I didn't have a place to live. I felt like such a failure.

"Do you know anyone at the church who can help me?" I asked. "I need help moving all my stuff." So, Melissa and another friend who was pregnant at the time said, "When you get everything situated, let us know, and we'll work on it from this end." So, Melissa said, "I'm going to call a couple guys from the church."

About an hour later, I rolled by this nice little place I found on Craigslist, and I noticed a number to call. I went and looked at it, and from then on, things moved very quickly. I rented a U-Haul. I had no idea how to drive a U-Haul, but I got this big old U-Haul and put it on my credit card. First, I went to the storage unit and got my belongings. Then, I went back to Kevin's and started putting what stuff I had there on the U-Haul. Then, I saw Kevin coming up. He started throwing things on the truck.

"I need to get out of here," I said. He was the last person who should have been putting stuff on the truck, but he just kept throwing things in and didn't say anything. I was in a daze. The neighbors next door were looking, but nobody said anything. I knew that once I left, I would never come back.

I found the place I wanted to rent. When I pulled up there, the owners took the deposit and the people from church moved in to help like I had never seen. Melissa came with four men from the church. They unpacked the U-Haul, brought it all in, and set up the kitchen and the bedroom like I'd been living there forever. I didn't have anything left to do. Melissa and another woman from Westside were putting things up in the kitchen, including the curtains. The men were doing the heavy lifting. I was blown away. I was at work on Monday. That was the bottom line. I had to be at school because the kids and teachers needed me, and I needed them.

Throughout this ordeal, I kept saying, "Nobody loves me, nobody loves me." Melissa interrupted me. "You have no idea. You have no idea. We love you. We are crazy about you. We are so glad that you're here and came into our lives." I had never really heard that from anyone before. I am forever indebted to her and still appreciate her friendship. I learned that I'm not the only one who's broken. There are so many broken people. Sometimes, you just have to remember—especially when you have been strong for so many people—that other people have had similar debilitating experiences. Now, I needed someone to be strong for me. Melissa said, "Why don't you lean on our shoulders and know that it will be okay?" And it was.

I felt like I had just covered up the problems in my marriage because everyone wants to be happily married and ride off into the sunset. But that wasn't the case, even when we were dating. It was like, "I know these chocolate chip cookies are bad for me, but I'm going to eat them anyway." So don't think a situation will turn out good just because you wish for it. I had not seen any examples of a good marriage. My models were my mother and her boyfriends. Her relationships were all about domestic violence, altercations and emotional abuse. I had never seen a healthy, loving relationship, so I didn't know what it looked or felt like. Even in my adoptive family, my adoptive mom and I didn't have a good relationship, so I wasn't really paying attention to how my parents interacted. Instead, I was focused on communicating that my real mom was my most important parent.

One of the hardest things in my life that I had to learn was, "It's okay to say, 'I need help.'" I never said that before, but I didn't have anywhere to turn. I thank God for Melissa and Westside Christian Church. It was divine intervention when she texted me at 7 a.m. that morning, asking how I was doing. I was in a dire situation. When you're in the community in a prominent position, people often think, "Well, you are supposed to be in charge and showing us how to do things." And I would think, *No, you have no idea of the hell I'm sitting in right now. Somebody please come and help me!* I had never asked for help before. But this time, I did. Church friends stepped up. From that point on, I started seeing a therapist.

"You can be very impactful," the therapist said. "You have to slow yourself down and always question these situations before you get into them." But, of course, I didn't listen to her. My mother always said, "Slow down, Kim. You're moving too fast; you're moving too fast!" I know I get into these situations where I get in trouble. I know that's one of the things I need to work on—I move too fast. My mom was trying to get me to slow down and process a situation before I got involved in it. I don't do that, especially when it comes to relationships.

I asked myself, *What are you running from? What are you running from?* Then I remembered that I didn't need to run from anything; I could take charge of my own life.

Even after moving back to Flint to accept a job as assistant superintendent in a nearby school district, I saw Kevin. I thought maybe we could work out the problems we had as a married couple. But I soon realized that it was not going to happen.

Looking back, I see that I was looking for love in all the wrong places. That unpleasant experience taught me a lot about myself and my longing for a close relationship. I told people, "Don't ask me anything about relationships because I'm the wrong person to ask about that." I saw myself as a loyal person to a fault and a hard worker. I have a lot of good qualities, but also a lot of things to remind me that I'm never to the point where I say, "Okay, you've arrived." In any case, I'm not a person who sits back and has regrets because everything happens for a reason in my life. With my marriage, I just wish I had been in a better place to make a better decision, but that's what I thought would work at the time. Because of the help from my friends, I was able to move on and learn from the whole experience.

I am perfectly imperfect and powerfully resilient. I accept and love all of me; I hope you will learn to do the same. God is not through with us yet!

EPILOGUE

After moving back to Flint, all my brother and I had to do was look at our mother, and we could see she was getting sick again. It's painful each time it happens. Ever since I was young, I've endured this pain, and it only gets worse as I get older. My brother called to say mom had another psychotic attack the Sunday evening before Thanksgiving. Once again, he had not even called an ambulance. I rushed to my mother's house that I bought for her with my savings so she would have a nice place in a decent neighborhood. When I got there, my mother held a knife while trying to light things on fire. Her history of setting fires and stabbing her boyfriend meant I had to act fast.

Waiting for the ambulance, my mom had two more seizures and then a third in the emergency room. She was hospitalized until the day before Thanksgiving, when a social worker brought her to my house. My brother and I ordered food for the holiday, so no one had to make special preparations for dinner. Although we had hoped for a typical meal, it was clear that my mother was still not doing well. Her eyes were bloodshot. Her hands trembled, and her speech slurred. Yet, over the weekend, she recovered enough so that I could settle her again in her own home.

I still have my real mom in me. When I was growing up, people would always say, "You're just like your mom; you're just like your mom." And there are certain qualities and characteristics about her that I'm glad that I have, especially just being strong. You may think, "How can anybody who's an alcoholic with mental illness be strong?" I remember one day I went over to her apartment. I just started crying. I knew she was getting sick. I called my sister and asked, "You talked to Mom? You know she's getting sick?" You could tell by her voice that she was getting ready mentally and emotionally to go to another place. I would just sit there and cry. My mom looked at me and said, "Don't cry." That was a sign of her love. "Don't cry." She wasn't crying. Who knows what was going on inside her head? Probably a sign of love that I needed to capture.

I knew that there had to be a better way out. All the educational opportunities that I had, K-12 and higher education, especially my experiences at Michigan State University, really shaped and molded me into the person I am today.

Growing up the way I did—with a mother who was bipolar, schizophrenic, with depression and mental illness, how could

I accomplish as much as I have? I keep asking myself that question. I have found some answers, but I continue to search for more because my family's characteristics didn't bode well for my siblings and me. I tell people we don't die from cancer, diabetes, heart problems or high blood pressure. We don't have those. People in my family who have died—as far as I know—killed themselves drinking.

I have an emotional hole in me—a hole like the one you dig in the ground. People say you won't fall in; however, the hole in me comes from not knowing whether my mother loved me as I grew up and even through most of my adulthood. Sometimes, I wonder, *Why do you have this hole in you because there have been good times, too?* Yes, but I wish I had more of those good things. I don't remember any birthday parties with kids, candles, and things like that. I still have many gaps in my memory about my childhood. I think I have suppressed them because they hurt too much to let them surface.

I still wonder who my real dad is. What's his side of the family like? Mama would stare at me, and I'd ask, "What are you looking at, Mama?"

"You're just like those people," she said, referring to my dad's family. But she never wanted to go into details about my dad. I know she said that his mom was a teacher, which I thought was interesting. And that he has a sister who lives in a close-by city. So, I know I have more family. I know it's not just all my mom in me. There's a heck of a lot of her and some of my father's side to consider. I don't know what that side is. I guess you could say I'm mysterious. I used to think about that a lot. It doesn't bother me as much as it used to, but it's still there in my thinking and feelings. All this stuff swirls inside me as I muddle my way through.

I have been back in Flint for several years now. After Kevin and I divorced, I knew I needed to move away from that environment and the memories. Flint was home to me. When I first came back, I accepted a position as an administrator of a private charter school in Flint. Still, when I got there, I found out that the school was not viable. It simply was not operating in a workable way, and I knew it was bound to fail. I did not have the same vigor, energy and passion for the work as when I was principal at Harvard Park.

My relationship with my adoptive father continued, but his life had changed. I thought about his long fight over the past ten years battling poor health. The first time I saw him in his sickness, it bothered me a lot and I never spoke of it again. I was used to seeing this hard-working, strong man who didn't need to lift weights or work out to stay fit, but now, he had changed. Unfortunately, he died a year after I returned to Flint. It was the most significant loss I had ever felt in my life.

Despite the poverty and hardship that I endured growing up, I was determined to keep my head above all the water. I was bright, stubborn, and increasingly ambitious. These qualities helped me develop leadership skills that eventually led to success as a teacher and educational administrator. Innate empathy kept me connected to students, teachers and other colleagues whose hardships were similar to those I confronted daily. I listened to their stories and tried to help them if I could. I took on responsibilities for seeing that my mother and siblings were doing as well as possible. They all had their own lives, so I tried to ensure they were alright. I always found help for my mother when she could not function.

Despite the mediocre grades I earned during my K-12 school years and as an undergraduate at Michigan State University, I loved school. It was a safe place where I could escape my family problems by becoming engrossed in reading. Teachers were my role models and my mentors. So, it is not surprising that I became a teacher and even aspired to be a school superintendent—not just because the school environment was a comfort to me. I thought I could offer students, teachers and other school district employees a similar sense of belonging. From my earlier experiences and barely average grades, who would have predicted that I would get three graduate-level degrees to do all this?

Some days, I wonder why I ever decided to be an educator. I don't make the money I wanted to when I was young, and the terrible things that happen to kids in our schools just make me sick. But then, I realize that although my life has been a mix of trials and triumphs, I have always been keen on helping others learn. Since I can relate empathetically to students of color who come from low-income homes like I did, I know how to hold them to high standards while also recognizing what they need to succeed in school. I am unapologetic in pursuit of excellence, equity and equality for all students. Wherever I go, in whatever capacity or position I hold, I want people to know that children come first—period!

When I first returned to Flint, I had to persevere and confront my problems yet again. My determination prevailed, and I am well. Perseverance has been a key to my success. I found mentors or they found me when I needed to be guided in constructive directions. I hope that my life story will inspire other people who grew up in similar circumstances as mine to hone their talents and abilities as they work toward their goals. I also want my story to encourage people who could act as mentors to someone like me to take action.

So many different dynamics interact within me. I live with and carry hurt, anger, pain, and resentment with me, but that does not stop me from being the person I am. I'm not perfect; I tell people, "I have issues!" My glass is always half full, and I can always work on getting the other half full. The other thing I like to tell people is, "I don't want it to get too full. I always like to have a little hunger in my belly because it causes me to work harder to reach my goals." I never like to be comfortable—I know that's both good and bad.

My motto is, "Don't get too full and don't get too comfortable. That's probably because of how I grew up. You never want to get too full and get too comfortable because you never know when you'll have to pack your bags and keep it moving."

My inner drive to help disadvantaged children has never lagged. People who know my work have said that my ability to work out a vision is one of my greatest attributes. I can picture the idea I aim for and then work hard to make it real. For example, as principal at

Harvard Park, after a year of planning, I established a dress code that resulted in students and parents respecting the school as a place of profound teaching and learning. The rise in Harvard Park's state test results is evidence of the positive effects of the changes I made in the school.

One of the things that I now understand is that I have become a mentor to others. I can see when someone has difficulty, whether a friend, colleague, relative or stranger. I try to offer help and support. Sometimes, I am accepted; other times, I can tell that I'm not to become involved. I'm disappointed then because I see a person who does not recognize that I'm trying to support them. But my efforts are a way to pay forward the mentoring I have received over the years. Sometimes, the person I'm trying to help takes advantage of me, or my help is not what they need. Other times, there is success. I'm learning that continued support is necessary for me to provide. I have learned from what others have done for me.

Although my life is unique to me and my circumstances, my living in poverty, racial prejudice, injustice, failing schools, poor health care, alcohol, drug addiction and the myriad other aspects of a life lived in need are not unique. Too many children and adults are caught by these afflictions. My response to such circumstances was to push against them—to take control of what I could, recognize and learn from my mentors, and believe I could achieve whatever I set my mind to. My life circumstances became a foundation for me to construct different outcomes for myself as an adult and help others do the same for themselves. My empathy for children who shared similar life conditions helped me make decisions about their misbehavior that would support their social, emotional and psychological growth rather than perpetuate punishing them, in a sense, for being who they were.

My mantra, "You don't get a free pass because you're poor," permeates my high expectations for children and adults. To do otherwise is the worst injustice we can do to children of poverty. I tell people, "Don't give up on them, whether they are the children in foster homes, juvenile systems, or single-parent homes. Whether they are Black children, brown children, white and yellow children, skinny kids, big kids, squirmy kids, kids with autism, gifted kids, creative kids, or kids from homes filled with alcoholism, mental illness, hopelessness, and despair. Whether they are homeless children or physically and emotionally abused children. Whether they include those with limited sight and hearing impairments, physically challenged children, or the child in a wheelchair. Don't give up on the marginalized kids—we need to give all of them a fighting chance."

At this point in my life, the big question for me is, "Can I and will I tackle my personal issues in the same way I have faced the challenges in my professional life?"

I am a runner, physically, intellectually, and emotionally. When I started running track in high school, I discovered it was a perfect outlet for my pent-up energy, emotions and mental turmoil. I have continued running—physically doing marathons, emotionally working on building a stable and satisfying social life and mentally envisioning ways to shape learning experiences that address the needs of each and every child. I have run hard in each of these realms, becoming successful in many of my endeavors. The track in front of me is still long, however. But, like any race, I've always crossed the finish line.

I have not married again, but I now have a young daughter, Maya Rose, who is God's greatest gift. She is smart, beautiful, and funny. She is my superstar! Her father is a great dad and Maya's hero. I resigned from my position in Pontiac and became the Executive Director of Education and Talent, a division of the Flint and Genesee Group. The work connects me with many people in Flint who I would not otherwise have had a chance to meet and gives me a venue to continue supporting the education of our cities' children and adults.

I continue to run, even if it is just around the neighborhood where I live. While I run, I think about what I'm working on in my professional and personal life. I am confident that I can reach my professional goals as I continue to accept challenging positions where I can grow as an educator. And each time I run, I feel like I am gaining strength and durability in my personal life to soar to new heights. Finally, when you stop running, you realize you can also spread your wings and fly!

ABOUT THE AUTHOR

Where many see desolation and destitution, Dr. Kimberly Leverette sees the enormous potential for hope, healing and wholeness. As a community advocate for underrepresented youth and young adults, author and speaker, Dr. Leverette serves as a walking epitome of what greatness unleashed looks like when one is cultivated in the right environment. Up from the ashes of an environment of alcoholism and anger, she soon found the power of mentorship—transforming her pain into purpose and helping others to do the same.

After being removed from a dysfunctional family, Dr. Leverette was thrust into the whirlwind of foster care. Constantly feeling like she didn't fit into any room she walked into, she thought at one point she was the only one who had a family as dysfunctional as hers. But after seeing many others who had the same testimony, she made an intentional decision to mimic her many mentors instead of her parents' past. With the intervention of mentors, counseling and a lot of love, she worked hard to turn her anger into moments of opportunity—infusing hope into the minds and hearts of students through education.

Professionally, Dr. Leverette serves as Executive Director of Education & Talent of the Flint & Genesee Group. In her role, she oversees all programming under Education & Training, including YouthQuest, TeenQuest, Summer Youth Initiative, Career Edge, and Flint Promise. Holding both a Bachelor of Arts in Elementary Education and a Master of Arts in Curriculum and Teaching from Michigan State University, as well as a Doctor of Educational Leadership from Maryville University, Dr. Leverette was a pioneer in Flint Community Schools as a teacher and assistant principal. In addition, she served in the Pontiac School District as the assistant superintendent of curriculum and instruction, as well as an administrator with underserved youth for six years in Springfield, Illinois at various schools.

A faithful member of Delta Sigma Theta Sorority, Inc., Dr. Leverette has won several awards, including the Outstanding Educator Crystal Apple Award from Michigan State University; the Academic Improvement Award for Exemplary Gains in Performance on the Illinois Learning Standards; as well as the Shining Star Award for Outstanding Contributions to Springfield Public Schools, to name a few. With her professional and personal experience, Dr. Leverette chooses to lead with love before she places labels on her students. More than anything, her mission and mandate is to show students around the world that what can happen for her can happen for them—and she's properly preparing them their bright future ahead.

For speaking engagements or interviews, email kleverette1913@gmail.com or visit TheLeadLearner.com.

Made in the USA
Monee, IL
11 August 2022

11414161R00095